The Eternal Moment of Now

Inner Peace through Emergent Knowledge Processing

Matthew Hudson

The Eternal Moment of Now

Inner Peace through Emergent Knowledge Processing

Matthew Hudson

ISBN 978-1-916063-20-4

First Edition: 2020

Second Edition: 2022

Revision 1: 630 [Second Edition]

For more information contact: ekpub@self-alignment.com

Emergent Knowledge Publishing

43 Bromley Avenue, Whitley Bay, NE25 8TN

United Kingdom

Tweet This Book!

Please help Matthew Hudson by spreading the word about this book on Twitter!

The suggested hashtag for this book is #TEMONToday.

Find out what other people are saying about the book by clicking on this link to search for this hashtag on Twitter:

#TEMONToday

Dedicated to

Maya Jean Hudson and Harvey Lewis Hudson

May you bring into this world much

peace, love and happiness

and receive the same in kind

Contents

APPENDICES

"These are in fact the men who, possessed of clear minds and far-sighted spirit, are not satisfied, like the brutish mass, to see only what is at their feet, but rather look about them, behind and before, and even recall the things of the past in order to judge those of the future, and compare both with their present condition. These are the ones who, having good minds of their own, have further trained them by study and learning. Even if liberty had entirely perished from the earth, such men would invent it."

The Discours sur la servitude volontaire of

ÉTIENNE DE LA BOÉTIE

1548

Rendered into English by

HARRY KURZ

Emergent Processing

New and growing senses developing within my being,
   alive in a way not fully sensed before,
      a fullness, a beingness,
         the eternal moment of now.

How did I get here?
What journey ensued?
I went in and came out of a toy train,
   a light bulb and the doorway to God.
To acceptance, complete, of all the above.

I was caught between worlds,
   always on one side, in fear of the other.
And yet split or torn.
Am I really on both sides together?

Not knowing and fearing the who or what was obscured.
Then just listening and seeing the outside as in.

Hearing at last, the messages unceasingly offered.

Discovering the joy in the truth.
The humour and laughter of finding myself

Becoming whole again.

The fear of oneself is all that there is,
with that fear of becoming and knowing just who you are.

Now with the knowing of self,
of the truth behind all that there is.
The truth that is mine, that created all this.

Now empowered to do what I will and I wish.
Unpicking the matrix, entwined through time,
by our cultures, our ancestors, religions and all.

Unpicked and cleared, and seen as it is.
Illusions, distortions keeping the matrix intact

The joke of being just a self-made game,
in which we all hide.
Then hoping and praying,
we can find our self again.

March 2009

Acknowledgements

First and foremost my appreciation and deepest gratitude go to David Grove for it was his insight and genius that made all of this possible.

Much love for Pam Saunders for her endless support, love and for always being there; all of this, along with continuing to share so much of the wonderful work she has created and developed. My understanding of Emergence wouldn't be the same without her.

Caitlin Walker is deserving of so much especially for her steadfast faith, guidance and patience with myself, along with her application and continuing creativity in the field of Clean.

My deepest respect and thanks to James Lawley for helping me to bring further clarity and direction to this work, his extensive review and advice as a preserver of the Clean core has evolved this work into something I had not originally conceived before, for this I am most grateful.

The greatest of thanks to Michael McKinney for his expert eye in editing and his powerful skills as a story-teller in encouraging this engineer to explore and express this work in a new way.

Cei Davies Linn for her generosity in offering so much to me about the early days when Cei and David were developing Clean Language and 'The Wounded Child Within' work, as well as keeping me clear and distinct in my definitions and descriptions.

I wish to make special mention of Dawn Atkinson, Etsuko Suda, Nicky Johnston (for his notes and spotting my grammatical oversights), Cricket Kemp, Sioelan Tjoa, Nick Tay, Gordon Readman, Hans van Laake, Si Evans, Val Bolam and Simon Stanton for all their support, kind words and offerings. This book would not be what it is without you.

I am endlessly appreciative of all my clients and fellow travellers in learning who have shared in this work and given of themselves and their valued feedback to help enhance and evolve this work. There have been so many helpful people along the way that I couldn't possibly name them all.

And finally, my great appreciation to you for giving this work your valued attention. May it offer new insights and positive changes for your life and for the lives of those around you.

Credits

Pam Saunders

For the development of the 'Emerging Moving' process and her kind permission to print and share here, along with her indepth input in proofreading.

Roger Hudson

For the artwork presented throughout this book.

PublicDomainPictures

For the front cover image, see http://www.pixabay.com for more.

Welcome to this Guide

Matthew Hudson

"Hello and welcome traveller!"

This guidebook is your introduction to Emergent Knowledge and its application for accessing the wonderful state of Inner Peace.

It will offer you some effective exploratory techniques along with some recent advancements in the growing field of Emergence.

Sit back, relax and enjoy.

Introduction

Well, this guide has eventually found its way into your hands. Its journey has been a long one covering many years. I'd like to say it began in 2007 however, the essence of this guide is far older than that.

How this guide arrived in your hands right now may have been from your interest in inner peace, self-development, mindfulness, Emergent Knowledge (EK) or Clean Language, David Grove (The prime creator of Emergent Knowledge technology and Clean Language) or maybe just the idea that there is something to be gained from accessing the 'Eternal Moment of Now'. And, it could also be some, all of these or none.

Regardless, I trust that right now there is an interest in where this guide can take you and in what benefits and new understandings about life and yourself may be discovered from reading and applying the methods shown.

This book has been written so that anyone who has an interest in self-development, self-improvement or mindfulness may gain a grounding in the basic Emergent Knowledge models and then be able to utilise these and the associated techniques; these have been designed for encouraging growth and insight for the practising individuals own development, as well as for delivery from trained counsellors, coaches and therapists.

The actual implementation of the techniques in this guide

is key to gaining a deeper understanding of the material presented. It is not only beneficial but, I believe, quite important to have this tacit knowledge before attempting to help others achieve the same unique experience for themselves. As with all personal work, make sure you have permission from your client, partner etc. before you proceed in any of this work.

I hope that you as my reader will run through the examples and techniques as described so you may experience and learn something new about yourself. This would be like the rediscovery of an aspect of yourself along with a new understanding about your life that was not there before. This is achieved through application, no amount of theoretical models and explanations can provide this as the structure of your understanding comes from *you* and *your* life, not a generalised set of models.

Once you have comprehended the material and positively experienced the presented techniques you will have at your disposal some simple and effective methods of calming and clearing the mind of yourself and others when needed.

A core fundamental of Clean Language was developed by David as a response to clinician led processes, where his intention was to remove the therapist from the client's process. As he developed upon this idea in the developing field of Emergent Knowledge he began to utilise algorithms, set patterns of questions and processes, to enable the client to explore the structure of their own world and hence their presenting problem or issue.

It is the structure of these algorithms and some basic techniques developed to encourage a natural and balanced change within the individual that we will be looking at in this book.

These methods allow one to develop a deeper holistic view of oneself in relation to one's current condition, either through facilitated actions or, as David was intending, to be 100% self-facilitated.

This book is intended to be a step towards achieving this, providing a base knowledge and a set of basic processes to allow anyone to begin their own exploration in a gentle manner.

Note that in this book I reference Pam Saunders and Steven Saunders, they are the same person, Pam chose to adopt her full feminine form in 2015. When I reference Steven this relates to any work she carried out prior to 2015.

The Format of this Guide

Please note that I'm an engineer, not a story teller. Therefore, as much as I would like to offer it, this material isn't a collection of anecdotes and quips. It is a clear and concise presentation of the original EK models and basic processes in which to experience and learn about EK, though my key intention in publishing this book is so you may grow and learn a little bit more about yourself and also discover how to experience the 'Eternal the Moment of Now' for yourself.

In 'THEORY I', I present the core theory of David Grove's Emergent Knowledge, in this is also included: what is meant by 'The Eternal Moment of Now', the fundamentals of Emergent Knowledge and a brief description of the philosophy of Clean.

A distinction is made between Clean Language and Clean, as the philosophy or notion of Clean has become a concept that is now commonly used by practitioners and trainers.

A review of the facilitator's role and how this relates to guiding the client's attention is provided before we venture into 'PRACTICAL I' where two very simple EK processes are offered as practical exercises to practise the material from the first part and gain some experience of Emergent Knowledge.

In 'THEORY II', I move over into my own developments within the field of Emergence, these are to be considered separate and not within the boundaries of Grovian Emergent Knowledge which I have reserved for David's work. The use of the term Emergence here, as opposed to Emergent Knowledge is purposeful to make this distinction.

Here I will review and update the Iterative Pattern of Emergence (also known as The Power of Six) and also present a new model which aims to explore the interactive expressions of human behaviour, this model also provides us with a distinct description and definition for the 'Eternal Moment of Now', that moment where we may experience Inner Peace, so we now have a guide and measuring stick to help bring us to this wonderful state.

'PRACTICAL II' then follows where I offer two new interesting and valuable Emergent techniques. The first is based upon the presented model in 'THEORY II', the second is a simple yet powerful tool designed to release stuck attention and bring this back into the here and now.

Finally in 'THE FUTURE' we take a brief look at what can happen next for you on this wonderful journey.

I will reiterate the following information one more time:

In order to fully understand this work, the completion of the exercises and processes when presented is required, giving them your full attention.

About the Author

Matthew Hudson is a trainer and developer of Emergence and Emergent Knowledge theory and practice.

He began his journey in developing his understanding of the human condition at 12 years old, when he was investigating and researching psychical phenomena with his school friends and became interested in hypnosis in his teens.

As a keen reader and experimenter he developed his skills and knowledge in more therapeutic methods such as NLP (Neuro-Linguistic Programming), EFT (Emotional Freedom Techniques) and hypnotherapy. During his practice and training Matthew was introduced to David Grove's Clean Language. It was here that he became aware of the key element that had been missing from all the work he had previously studied and utilised:

"All the required answers to the client's presenting issues are already within the client and do not come from the facilitator."

Matthew became David's personal assistant in late 2007 and worked with him until his death in January 2008. During this time he was tasked with cataloguing and modelling David's final and pioneering work at that time, Emergent Knowledge.

Since then, he has published several articles on the basics of David Grove's Emergent Knowledge theory and methodology and continues to promote and share this information freely and with passion.

Matthew was later introduced to further developments of Emergence by Pam Saunders, who co-developed some of the original EK ideas with David. Pam's own developments and excursion from the Grovian methodology are known as 'The Holigral Method'.

This book is Matthew's first iteration in being an author.

Disclaimer

Although the Emergent Knowledge methodology was originally designed to work with clients in a therapeutic way, in this guide I am not presenting these processes as therapeutic methods. If you or those you are working with are in need of any therapeutic intervention for any issue(s) presented, do not use these techniques but seek professional advice. For everything else, it is your responsibility to look after your own well-being while using these techniques.

Here, the intended use of these techniques are for your own and others self-development, coaching and education. When working with others ensure you have their permission before you begin any intervention work.

If you choose to ignore the above advice and decide to use this material for your own or another's recovery from prior trauma - for instance you are a trained facilitator or therapist - you are accepting full responsibility for your own actions and through this you absolve the author of any liability for any repercussions from your actions.

Professional training in the theory and facilitation of Emergence and Emergent Knowledge is available on request. Please contact the author via email on:

matthew@self-alignment.com

THEORY I

- What is the Eternal Moment of Now?
- What is Emergent Knowledge?
- Fundamentals of Emergent Knowledge
- Role of the Facilitator and Client

What is the Eternal Moment of Now?

'Panta Rei'

Everything Flows

Mindfulness

The idea of an 'Eternal Moment of Now' has links to several fields. Perhaps the most notable link at the current time is to 'Mindfulness', which has recently become a household term, and, with the many books and courses available, there are an ever-increasing number of ideas and definitions. Though it should be mentioned that this idea of mindfulness is significantly older than our recent connection to it.

Fundamentally, it is that state of consciousness where we are fully attending to our experience in the present moment in time.

There may be many times during a day when our attention becomes absorbed in obsessive or upsetting thoughts about our past, or where we find ourselves anxious about the future. When our attention drifts away from what we are attending to in this moment we can lose our connection to who and where we are. These are the moments where we can really benefit from accessing the 'Eternal Moment of Now'.

Our response and understanding of the world is coloured by our personal interpretation of the experience. This interpretation is shaped by our history, present time analysis and unconscious responses. For instance, a previous traumatic incident can have life long repercussions and influence how we see the world afterwards. Some phobias, for example, arise in this way.

As we accumulate memories and the associated interpretations, we may no longer be encountering the world in the present moment. Rather, at times, we encounter a situation through a set of considerations, beliefs and an identity created through our past experience.

For example, suppose you've just started your first full-time job. On the third day, the boss sends for you and when you enter his office, he yells angrily that you've done something wrong, and he's so angry and incoherent that you're not even sure what's happening. That would probably stick in most people's memory. Then suppose, ten years and two jobs later, the boss sends for you. Your immediate reaction may be a spike in blood pressure, stomach churning, heart racing, sweating — because you are interpreting the present moment through that set of constructs, which were built on that past visit to a different boss's office.

Instead of being fully present, a portion of your attention is still stuck back in that previous experience. And, the reality is, your new boss just wants to compliment you on a well-done project.

Training our attention to come back to the here and now is a worthwhile pursuit which has been proven through research and experience to be a valuable tool for living and working in the 21st century.

Benefits of Being in the Present Moment

Regularly accessing this state of mindfulness has been shown to offer:

- Positive benefits for our health and happiness
- Reduction of stress
- Enhanced performance
- Better focus and clarity
- A deeper insight and awareness of self
- Improved creativity, memory and sleep quality

Having the personal experience of being in the present moment is the only real way to define mindfulness for yourself, as it is a unique and subjective experience.

A happy, peaceful client.

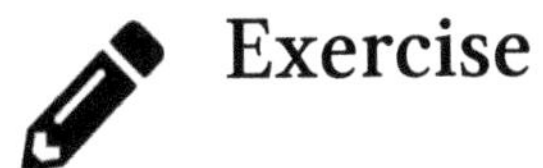

Exercise

And, where is your attention right now?

This short exercise is presented so you may notice what and where your attention moves to when no direction is given, other than the purpose of noticing what happens.

1. Sit or lie back and relax for a minute or two. If you wish to, close your eyes.
2. On bringing your attention back here, recall where your attention naturally moved to.

Was it a particular thought, feeling or memory?

____

____

And, where does that come from?

____

____

Review of Exercise

How much of your attention in this exercise was actually focused on simply being in the present moment?

Were you doing the exercise, but also had a part of your attention evaluating the presented material against your current ideas of reality?

Were there some doubts? Was there some internal self talk, deliberating the process, checking what was occurring?

Did a past memory appear?

Did a thought about the future appear?

All the above experiences are examples of our attention being taken away from simply experiencing being in the here and now. If you were aware of your awareness and comfortably tracking your attention then this was a brief moment of mindfulness, fantastic! If not, then at least you may now be aware of where your attention could be being distracted to.

These distractions from the present moment are what can stimulate our internal system to provide us with the fear, self-doubt and countless other psychological aberrations so many of us are subject to. We will also discover that these distractions and where they take us may actually be the resource we need to bring us to a resolution.

Intention Behind the EK Processes

The EK processes as presented in this book are designed to work directly with your attention: first to free it from these distractions, and then to bring your attention back to the here and now - helping to integrate you back into the 'Eternal Moment of Now'.

Emerging Moving (Process #1), is designed to help orientate us to where we are and what we're doing and feeling in the here and now when this loss of attention occurs.

The Six Steps (Process #2), is one of the most basic EK processes that David developed. It was designed as a starting process for the client to begin to explore their issue in greater detail with the intention of evolving new structures around it by utilising emergent processes. It is perfect for beginning facilitators and clients to gain an understanding of the fundamental processes.

These exercises and processes utilise several ideas and technologies of the mind, most notably Emergent Knowledge which we shall start to explore in the next chapter.

It is proposed that the exercises only require your attention and focus for a few minutes each to achieve a noticeable positive result, running the processes will require more of your time and attention, usually about 60-90 minutes.

Be assured it will be worth every moment, for the more energy and attention you are able to apply to these processes then the more gains and changes to your well-being will occur.

It is imperative that when self-processing or working with a facilitator your honesty and authenticity is fully intact, if you choose to hide, lie or attempt to deceive then the effectiveness of these processes will be reduced; you are only cheating yourself. Though it must be stated, if you do recognise these things beginning to occur, then acknowledge these urges and utilise them in the process in this way much information will emerge and changes will happen.

What is Emergent Knowledge?

> *"The emergence of knowledge via spatial and other transformations are thought experiments that take an issue or context and subject it to a series of observational perspectives, the purpose of which is to construct a metaphorical identity of the knowledge and its relational knowledge set, structural support and provenance."*
>
> David Grove

Introduction

Emergent Knowledge describes a theory and set of processes originally devised by counselling psychologist David Grove, which was formed as part of his development in Clean Language and Clean Space. Though, it became its own body of work towards the end of David's life.

Further development and insights were evolved during 2005-6 when David began co-developing these ideas with Steven Saunders, who has continued to take this work forward and created her own set of tools and techniques based on the principles discovered in this earlier work, when I utilise this work or terminology it will be explicitly stated.

Here in Theory I the fundamentals of EK from the Grovian perspective are presented, along with my own interpretations and developments later in Theory II.

EK processes create the conditions in which new, generative information emerges from within a client's psychological and physiological system. They use multiple iterations of a set of simple questions (algorithms), each of which invites the client to attend to a specific area.

In response to the emergent relationships and connections between the answers, the client's system spontaneously begins to restructure its understanding of the presenting issue.

This restructuring generally provides the client with a more holistic and encompassing model of the world and their place within it.

What Makes EK Different?

I've spoken with many friends and colleagues over the years about the work I and others do in the field of Clean and Emergent Knowledge. There has been a proportion of those people who held a view of therapy as something that was 'done to them' by someone who 'understood' their issues and could 'make sense of it' for them or even considered that the therapist was there to 'fix' them.

This had resulted for some of those I have spoken with, who were suffering with anxieties, to turn away from therapeutic intervention, as they believed that their experiences which had caused the suffering could not be understood by a therapist, and therefore could never be resolved by someone who had not gone through the same experience.

This idea of another needing the experience and knowledge is common, and continues to exist in many fields - for example, it may be observed in some areas of our social support services.

Please note that this statement absolutely does not seek to undermine any recognition from the highly motivated and determined individuals who have become clean from drugs or alcohol, got themselves off living on the streets, or dealt with their sexual abuse, and now work with similar vulnerable people to assist in guiding them out of their own current situation; it is simply a statement that recognises that change comes from within the individual, not from the outside.

Many a client has walked into the therapist's (also counsellor, coach or physician's) domain and walked out again feeling coerced, evaluated and even re-stimulated. This was a problem that David was keen to address with his work in Clean Language, to create a manner of working that would truly honour the client's system as it was in the moment that presented itself as the client began their session.

As his work was developing towards EK, there was a sense that even when using the original Clean methods an intention was still present that wasn't necessarily present within the client. Even asking the client, *"What would you like to have happen?"* infers that the client is wanting something.

Now it would be asinine to state that the EK facilitator is never influencing or has an intention, David was simply looking to create the conditions in which to minimise this as much as possible. Therefore we still ask the client the above question, or even some of the interesting alternatives which David proposed.

You will also see later in this volume, that I offer some very simple processes to be followed, though as one becomes adept in Emergent Knowledge processing these become more like a framework and a guide, for instance when I am working with a client in the transcripts I step outside the defined structure depending on the information being presented by the client. Note that in these moments I am always working within the client's developing model, not bringing in my own interpretations.

With the development and use of David's EK methods, those problems were reducing; his techniques allowed for the client's own inner expression to become that which created their own process.

It is as though the EK methodology sits meta (at a higher conceptual level) to the client's process itself and therefore stimulates the client into their own unique process, one built by them for them. In this way any changes made are by and through the client.

I see the use of EK methodology as potentially being a system of operating that could enable over 7 billion processes!

The Seven Elements of EK

There are several significant elements of EK which, when presented together, offer a unique approach:

1. Clean Facilitation: The facilitator utilises minimal intervention and non-invasive questions
2. Iteration: Asking a question or directing the client repeatedly, usually in sets of seven [1+six]
3. Reinterpretation: The action of interpreting something in a new or different manner
4. Representation: Representing the answer in an alternative form - as in Clean Space in which we translate the responses into a physical form, then place those representations in space
5. Navigation: Relating each representation (space) to the others
6. Algorithms: A defined set of questions and instructions to enable a client to inspect and explore their condition
7. Present Time: The questions are given in the present tense

The Emergent A to F Model

Before we look at each of the seven elements, let us take a look at the core model which is used throughout Emergent Knowledge. This model provides a workable map and baseline to understanding all the concepts presented.

Starting with A, then B

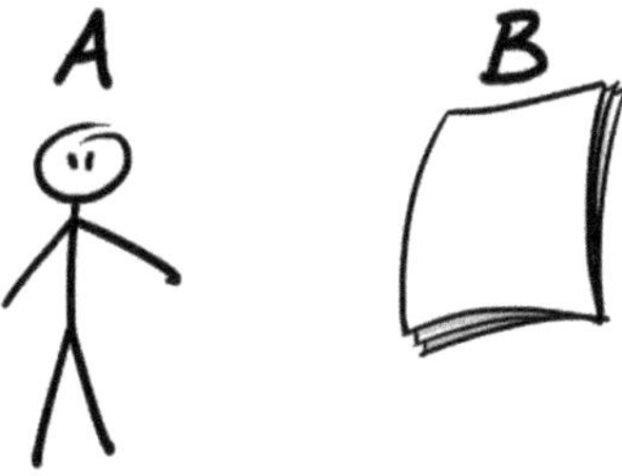

A and B

Generally, all training in EK begins with the above image and then proceeds to develop the deeper ideas out of this basic structure.

The client is shown in the above image to be at position A. Their stated issue or presenting condition is shown at position B.

Even though later we will be using 'real' space to isolate the issue (B), the separation of B from A here is purely conceptual to aid in the comprehension of the model and processes.

C for Current Context

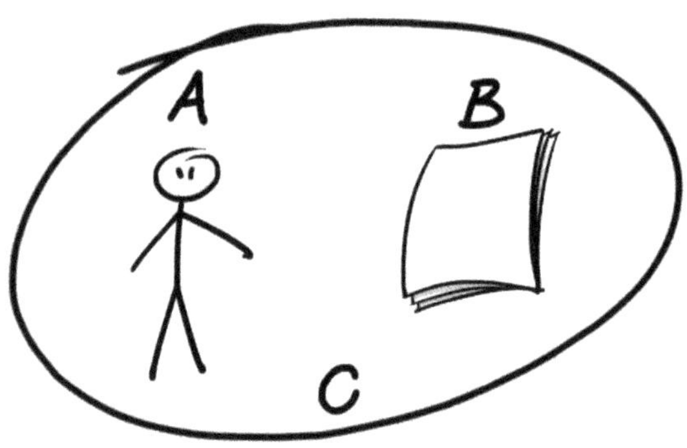

The Client's ABC World

There are two aspects to C:

1. The Space of C - the boundary encompassing both A and B creates an area known as the space of C. This is representative of the client's current world-view, i.e. what they are currently aware of with respect to themselves (A) and their issue (B).
2. The Boundary of C - representative of all the rules and constructs that the client (A) has adopted to maintain this world-view.

The Space of C is also known as the 'Problem Space'. It is the client's current paradigm. Later we will see how our paradigms can change depending on our experience.

D for multi-Dimensional

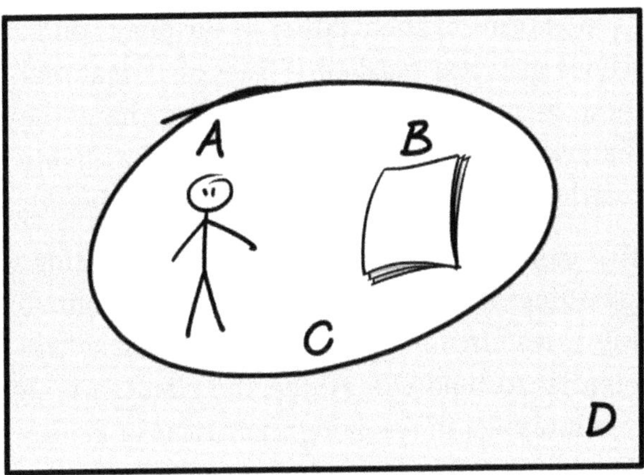

The Space of D

The area outside of C has been called 'The Space of D' and also the 'Potential Space'.

Diagrammatically, we can see that D is everything that is outside of C; therefore, it is everything that the client is currently **unaware** of with respect to their ABC system. In this manner it is proposed that in the current moment, the constraints of C are holding back the information held within D.

This information could be completely unconscious, as well as just out of awareness. For instance, a client is upset about how their father treated them and suddenly left when they were young, in the beginning of the session all the focus is on the negative aspects of this relationship (Space of C material) this is all laid out and acknowledged utilising the Emergent Knowledge methods, then during the session the client's memories of their father at birthdays and coming to a school play are recalled (Space of D material). Note that these memories have always being there, they have for whatever reason not been recognised as being in the same world-view or category of 'bad father' before.

Note that calling D a 'Space' can be a little limiting to fully understanding what is held in D. It was originally seen as being a resourceful space for the client, where it has the potential to hold everything the client is required to know with respect to resolving their issue at B. This comes from David's work in Clean Space, and it is here that we encounter a mixing of metaphors.

Due to this mix, there is a requirement for a clear distinction between the logical structures of Emergent Knowledge and the working metaphors of Clean Space.

Pam Saunders proposed the idea that D is in fact the Time element. I have extrapolated this to offer D to be of a multi-'D'imensional nature, where it provides the potential to view multiple times (actual and alternative pasts, presents and futures), multiple spaces, multiple viewpoints and even multiple universes with respect to the client's original issue. Conceptually we allocate these as coming from D, as they were not originally present in C when we began - once recognised they become resident within C.

Anything is possible in D; clients may access information

from other dimensions (alternative universes or planes of existence). From David's Wounded Child work, the child 'frozen in time' is in another dimension to the one the client is currently in, and hence the messages being received from there do not immediately translate or make sense. However, once a client recovers this aspect of self, these messages and their effects are fully understood, usually with great relief and wonder.

There is no limit to what the client can access in D - in this way it reflects both Pam's 'Time' and David's 'Resourceful' space, as well as opening up further possibilities.

E for Emergence

We also have E, which is the emergence of new information and understanding, which develops in the spaces of A, B and C. The starting conditions for E to occur are when there are sufficient new links and relationships forming within C, sometimes additional information from D is required to enter into the space of C.

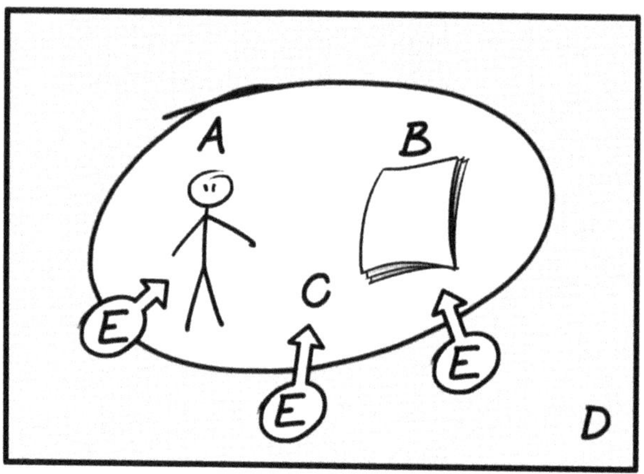

Emergence Manifesting through A, B and C

It is here when all this new information comes into a new **relationship** with the existing information, that the boundary conditions of C begin to deconstruct or untie, as they are no longer valid.

As stated, the required information may already be present in C, it just hasn't been fully integrated yet, or the as yet unrecognised information from D must become known and understood in the current context.

This is a complicated scenario with many facets to it. The core structure though, is that through this complexity and the interplay of all the presenting factors a new higher-level organisation spontaneously occurs, generally bringing relief.

We can also think about this as at the moment that A becomes aware of something in D, that part (+d) is synthesised into the existing structure, a new boundary for C is evolved to encompass this new information.

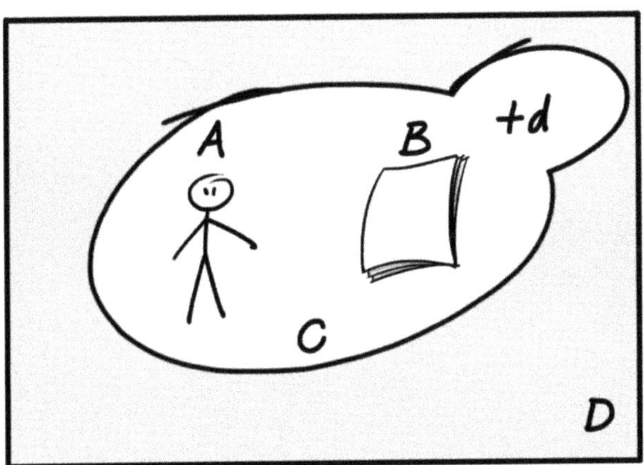

The Space of 'C' Expands

Emergence then, enables the new space of C to stabilise. It consists of a new set of constructs, predicates and understandings. The new space of C and its corresponding boundary represent the revised operational paradigm for the client.

In summary, prior to E emerging the boundary conditions of C are deconstructed - i.e. the old way of thinking dissolves - and E manifests when this boundary is rebuilt, expanding out the space of C a little more into the potential area of D.

F for Facilitator

Finally we encounter F, the facilitator, who remains outside of everything. This is why F is shown outside of D. Anytime that the facilitator brings themselves into the client's world, they are entering into the client's A to E world; when the facilitator begins to offer suggestions and their interpretations, they are disrupting the client's system, and potentially bringing aspects of D into C that have no residence there from the client's perspective.

The Full A to F Model

'Facilitate' has the definition: **make (an action or process) easy or easier**. It comes from the Latin *facilis* meaning 'easy, easily accomplished'.

A key criterion for the Clean facilitator is to assist the natural evolution of the client's system without directing or distorting it. David often said that this required the skill of a good midwife - *mid* originally meant 'with' and *wife* 'woman', thus 'person with woman'. A good midwife works with the mother, taking their cue from the baby's need to be born and the mother's need to give birth to the baby.

This requires facilitators to be unusually receptive: sensitive to small, sometimes subliminal indications. People need much less overt intervention than many of us realise. Generally they know for themselves, at least when asked the right questions, what is good for them.

David said that the use of Clean Language (and now Emergence) "...creates a protective temporal and spatial womb or matrix in which *the facilitator's* job is to be a good midwife, and to recognise and develop and assist in the birthing of new information which is born out of..." the clients language, behaviour and ongoing experience.

Defining Moments

Following on from Emergence and our A to F model is the question of how come we (at A) found ourselves stuck with a problem (at B), in the space of C to begin with?

Putting it simply, this is due to living life and naturally, or unnaturally, experiencing defining moments throughout.

These are named Defining Moments, as it is these *moments* when our life is interrupted to such a degree that we must shift who we are, and the changes we make in this shift *define* who we become.

A defining moment is made up of two distinct parts:

An Interruption	A moment where what one intended or expected to occur, was hindered or interrupted in some manner.
A Shift	When the *interruption* was intolerable to such a degree that one had to shift and become different in some way so as to make the moment tolerable.

This definition infers that any interruption or hindered moment which someone experiences is a potential defining moment, and it is, however this is wholly dependent on the individual's resilience or ability to handle that moment.

And our ability to be resilient then, is based on how rich and varied our life choices and opportunities have been to support and develop our internal systems to adapt and change to the ever changing environment. Charles Darwin stated, *"It is not the strongest of the species that survive, nor the most intelligent, but the one more responsive to change."*

Pam in her book, The Emperor's New Psychology, offers us the following:

"...these aspects are created by defining moments within the personal life, where the structure of the personal collective changes, due to the personal measurement made of the defining moment."

And, *"In a defining moment a shock interrupts the smooth flow of awareness, and the person has to re-project awareness due to the interruption. The old sensing awareness remains frozen exactly where it was in space and time."*

Here follows an example of a defining moment shift in poetry form (or perhaps even the lyrics to a song...)

Falling to Pieces

I'm falling to pieces
Something ripped right out of me
I'm being torn to pieces
Only half the man I used to be

You're taking over my will
I'm cowering here and waiting
As you deliver your strike
My heart breaks away
My heart breaks away

That moment, that splitting moment
The cold hard shock, not once, but twice
Cold, dark, emptiness, ringing throughout my being
My thinning blood runs cold as ice

Who am I?
What have I become?
I loved and enjoyed this life
I've gone, I am no more.

With nothing left to fight with
I fell and I succumbed
To your force and your denials
  of the world I knew before

I've fallen into pieces

Something ripped apart from me
These fragments drop away
Now only half the man I used to be

The other half's not me
Who have I become?
Inside now filled with anger
Where is all this fear from?

Is the tormented now the tormentor?
How does this pain find a way
  to release the oppressed and the oppressor?
Has this pain only got one way?

I've fallen into pieces
My true beingness ripped right out of me
Torn into tiny pieces
Only half the man I used to be

An Example of Resilience

Consider two children, both of which are playing on a swing in a play park. The swing breaks and both children fall and hit the ground. One of the children looks up and starts to laugh, thinking, "Wow, that was exciting!", the other child becomes distraught and begins to cry, thinking, "There's no one here to help me, I'm hurt and all alone! I'm never going on the swings again."

They both had a very similar experience, however their responses are very different and have a direct effect upon their well-being. Depending on the situation for our second child, different kinds of shift may occur.

In the future when both children enter a playground, our first child simply runs with excitement to the swing, whereas our second child tightly holds onto mother and may now have reservations about joining in the fun.

The Shift

> *"Trauma is an impingement from the environment and from the individual's reaction to the environment that occurs prior to the individual's development of the mechanisms that make the unpredictable predictable."*
>
> Donald W. Winnicott

Each time we make a shift and change ourselves due to defining moments we are recreating the boundaries of C, and each time this occurs these new boundaries are created within the existing boundaries, thus causing the size of the Space of C to perpetually reduce. This is a full inversion of the process described for Emergence, where the boundary expands out to create more space for C, a model for increasing awareness.

We are therefore consistently reducing our abilities and level of current awareness each time we are required to shift due to these defining moments. For it is through this process that we become increasingly less and less aware of our sense of 'who we really are' and increase the distortions of that which we perceive.

These changes affect our sense of self: a shift from who we were before to who we are afterwards. There is then a prior identity and a post identity. It is these identities that we connect with and explore, with the intention of retrieving the earlier ones and bringing them up to present time to be reintegrated into the present self.

Each identity is an amalgamation of purposes and characteristics which were formed to handle the defining moment at the time, this identity is then adopted and unknowingly retained. Each identity is created and perpetuated by the individual, not by anything or anyone else, therefore it is only the person themselves that may resolve each and every trauma.

This piece may look to be painting Defining Moments in a bleak and cold light, deep trauma may have all the effects described, though as you will see in the next section these moments also open up the opportunity to grow and become stronger.

In life, no matter what happens, or how well protected we are, Defining Moments will occur. There is also another set of **Positive Defining Moments** that may occur in life where through them life becomes more *tolerable* and they enhance and strengthen our sense of self, such as finding our 'Soulmate' or achieving a lifelong goal.

The A to F Model and The Defining Moment

Just as we have utilised the A to F model to aid in our understanding of how Emergence occurs, we can apply the same model to the defining moment.

- A - Person
- B - Purpose / Intention / Expectation
- Space of C - What is known in the 'here and now'
- Boundary of C - Rules and structures required to maintain A's world-view
- D - That which is outside of A's current awareness with respect to A & B

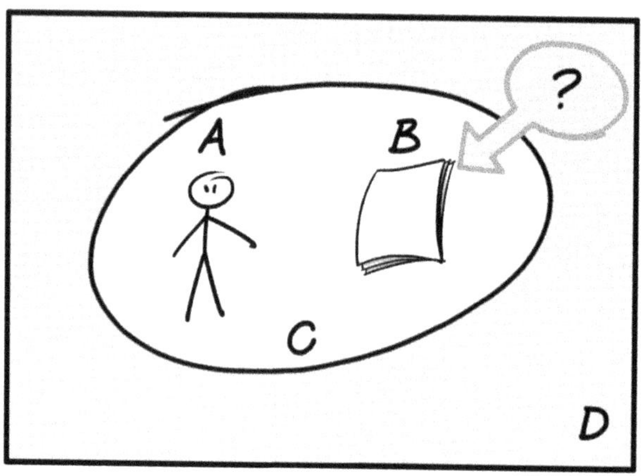

A to F Model for a Defining Moment

In a defining moment there is a 'projection' from D into the Space of C, which is of sufficient magnitude to interrupt B.

A now has two potential routes to manage this:

1. The interruption is categorised and understood as part of the existing world-view, in this regard A adapts the boundary conditions of C to accommodate. The Space of C grows a little and A's awareness increases proportionately. In essence, a natural occurrence of emergence in action.

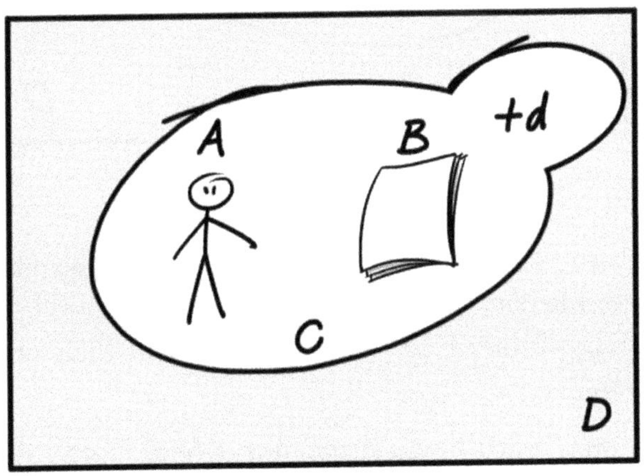

Natural Emergence

2. The interruption cannot be understood as part of the existing world-view; here the boundary conditions of C have to be broken. Through doing this, A's world-view is no longer valid and now has to be rebuilt to accommodate this change. Notice that this is a failure of A's existing belief structures and view of the world.

Here is the source of 'not feeling good enough', 'not fitting in', fear, lack of self-belief etc..

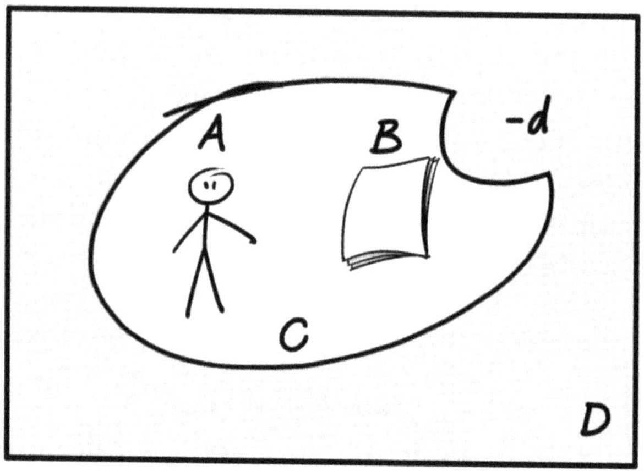

Awareness Reducing

The restructuring that occurs in the second route adds more rules and beliefs than existed before. It therefore becomes even more limiting to the individual than their previous structure.

Sometimes reaching a crisis point, where more rules and structures are put in place are a requirement to make the steps out of that crisis manageable. And once the crisis is over, one may then be able to grow, adapt and step outside of requiring these rules and structures anymore.

Evolutions of Thought

In an Emergent Knowledge session the occurrence of emergence appears in various ways. Here are some examples of how a client may suddenly come to realise something new about what they are working on:

- When a collection of seemingly unconnected memories brings a new perspective on all the memories and ideas and the client is able to see how they all interconnect.
- When the client's viewpoint or perspective of a particular memory or category of ideas is flipped or reinterpreted to mean something else.
- When a forgotten memory comes back into awareness which defines and explains the existence of the existing condition.

Moments of emergence are not always of a revelatory nature, sometimes we just get a glimmer of new information, something peeks through and we're only just able to capture it. For instance, this could be a strange sensation not noticed before, an odd image or sound in the mind, a repeated statement or word, a gasp or a short intake of breath. All of these are potential targets for the client or facilitator to attend to.

Although this appears to be a small step, it is actually a giant leap; as this new piece of information becomes a part of the client's developing network it will be further explored and will begin to fully reveal itself through further iterations. David proposed that the client's symptoms were unsuccessful attempts by the mind and body to heal itself, thus the therapist's job is to create a suitable context in which they can encourage these symptoms to be successful.

The existence of this new information, especially when inverse, alongside the original knowledge of the system can put the system out of balance. The architecture of the whole system now needs to adapt to accommodate it.

Fundamental Elements of Emergent Knowledge

> *"A new type of thinking is essential if mankind is to survive and move toward higher levels."*
>
> Albert Einstein

In our previous chapter I introduced the seven elements of Emergent Knowledge. This chapter discusses each of these in greater detail.

You may notice that each element naturally leads on to the next.

1. Clean Facilitation

What is Clean?

Clean is a core aspect and method of working which permeates all the intervention work we perform in Emergent Knowledge. It has become a way to describe a manner of operating with a client, separate from the term Clean Language. Though, in referencing Clean Language it is now common to hear both terms used interchangeably.

3 Core Guidelines of Clean are:

- Facilitators remove themselves from the clients process whenever and wherever possible.
- Facilitators actions are performed so that any contamination of the client's process is kept to a minimum.
- Facilitators only reference elements which have already been introduced by the client or to relationships with respect to those elements.

The client must be allowed to come to their own truth of the matter they are attending to and not have anyone else's thoughts, interpretations and ideas pushed on to them.

A Brief History of Clean

The concept of working Clean with a client was developed by David Grove during his work in the 1980s with his

Clean Language technique. This technique was designed to help clients discover and develop their personal symbols and metaphors during psychotherapy sessions to aid in the resolution of a prior trauma.

Clean Language utilised a particular set of questions which David had refined to reduce how much a facilitator could influence the client's process with their own interpretations, metaphors etc.

These questions when used, predominantly included an aspect of the client's recent communication in order to maintain the client's attention on the developing awareness of their experience.

For example a client states, "I'm upset about her decision."

Clean Language responses to this could be:

- *"And what kind of 'upset'?"*
- *"And is there anything else about that 'upset'?"*
- *"And what happens just before 'her decision'?"*
- *"And where could 'her decision' come from?"*
- *"And that's 'upset' like what?"*

Staying Clean in Session

For our purposes here if you have not yet received any formal Clean Language training it is recommended that you just use the EK questions and instructions as presented, do not add-in anything else or take anything away, there is no need to over-think what is happening here or query the why's and wherefore's - the technicalities will come out later. Be assured that these questions are designed with the same purpose and usage as David designed the original Clean Language questions, thus protection and a client-centric purpose are evident.

Newcomers, stick to the above advice and the 3 Core Guidelines of Clean and all will be fine. When you do find the opportunity, locate and visit a Clean Language training facility for training in this area.

More Information on Clean

For more information on Clean Language there are many sources available - see Appendix 1 for websites and books. I would highly recommend accessing this material to gain a solid grounding in the root source of Emergent Knowledge.

Please note that although EK grew out of Clean Language, it is in a different category of process structures than that which Clean Language is predominantly known for, metaphor development and symbolic modelling. The questions and methods utilised in EK are still very much within what is considered to be Clean Language, non-invasive and non-presumptive as already presented.

James Lawley offers some insight here about this notion of Clean Language, *"In my memory, David rarely referred to Clean Language as 'method', I think he saw it as more of a 'means'. The questions that were included in Clean*

Language got extended over the years, each time he needed a new 'means' to facilitate a new process."

Clean Language then, did not stop in 2002 when he started experimenting with Clean Space, this was simply a continuation and the same developmental shifts occurred with the advent of Emergent Knowledge.

In EK there may be some use of the classic Clean questions to elicit more information about aspects of the client's world, however, these are not the driving force behind the processes.

> *"Clean Language is the art of asking questions so that you as a therapist do not contaminate or impose a model of the world upon your client."*
>
> David Grove

2. Iteration

Exercise

Before we begin this section, I'd like for you to complete this short exercise: [note that each question asked relates to the original answer in Step 1.]

1. Write down something that you'd like to work on or explore.

____

2. *"And, what do you know about that?"*

____

3. *"And, what else do you know about that?"*

____

4. *"And, what else do you know about that?"*

____

5. *"And, what else do you know about that?"*

____

6. *"And, what else do you know about that?"*

____

7. *"And, what else do you know about that?"*

____

8. *"And, what do you know now?"*

____

Keep your answers close by as you will be referring back to these in the following section.

The Iterative Pattern of Emergence

Through the development of Emergent Knowledge, David began to notice a structure to the language clients used as they ran his processes. Asking a simple question repeatedly, provided some very interesting results. David observed clients in the USA, UK and in France and found that even across cultures the structures proved to be consistent.

To test his hypothesis he created a thought experiment where he limited his questions to the point that they would test if this pattern was observable and repeatable. The questions utilised were:

"What do you know about that?" and then

"And, what else do you know about that?" asked five times and finally

"And, what do you know now?"

David had noticed that each question brought with it a particular structure to the response. Here follows that pattern as observed; each response forms a new stage in the pattern.

Stage 1 - Proclaim

The client at A on their first question will **Proclaim** their problem.

This is shown as B in the A to F Model.

Proclaim

Client: *"I'm always getting nagged at."*

Stage 2 - Explain

On the second iteration the client usually **Explains** what was said in Stage 1. This will most likely include their personal experience with the narrative of the problem.

Here the client brings A and B into relationship with each other.

Explain

Client: *"She gives me a headache, with all this nagging and shouting."*

Stage 3 - Reinforce and Expand

With the third iteration, the client will **Reinforce** the explanation from Stages 1 and 2, although now the scope of their language will be moving towards the global nature of the problem. The client is **Expanding** and **Reinforcing** the original issue, providing evidence and structure to what is happening.

In our model, the client has now encompassed A and B with the boundary C. The space of C contains the contextual information.

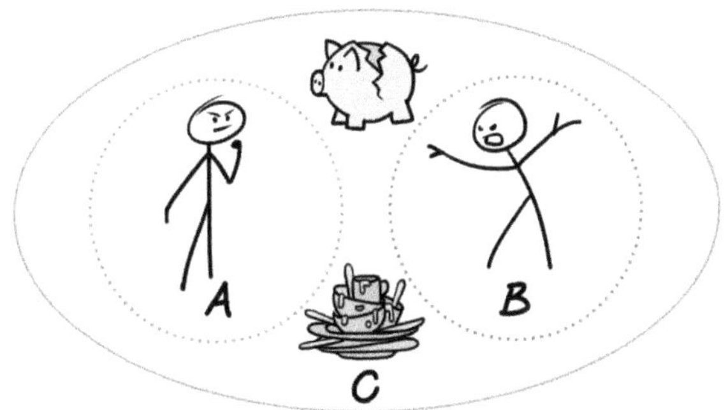

Reinforce

Client: *"I just want some peace and quiet to fix my bike up, but I'm told to clean up or that we don't have the money. It's a constant barrage of nagging!"*

"She is really annoying and it makes me angry and frustrated."

Stage 4 - The Wobble

The fourth iteration starts with the reinforcement of Stage 3, but then we get **The Wobble**. At this point there is a pause, and doubt about the issue enters in. The facilitator waits for the doubt. It will usually be the opposite commentary to what we have just heard, this is referenced as being Not B or !B as it manifests as the inverse of B.

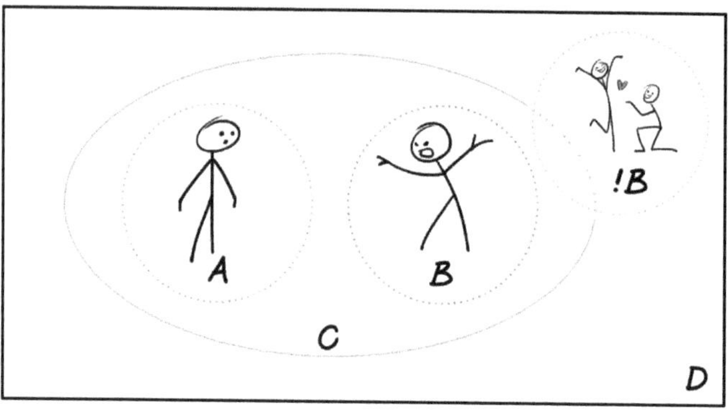

The Wobble

Client: *"I just really feel like leaving sometimes... but, then... well I suppose I'd miss her really."*

"And, it's not always shouting to be honest. I remember when we got married that was a great time, why can't it still be like that?"

This opposite commentary enters in at the edge of C, from the space of D. For this to occur the boundary of C has to open up, like a portal, to this area of potentiality (D).

Stage 5 - Crash and Burn

As we move into the fifth iteration, the client really begins to heat up on the inside as their world-view is shifting. How can they be stating two binary opposite statements (B and !B) in the same answer during Stage 4?

This stage was named **Crash and Burn**, as it is the stage where the prior structures of the issue are no longer valid and these 'collapse to the ground'. This may confuse and disorientate the client.

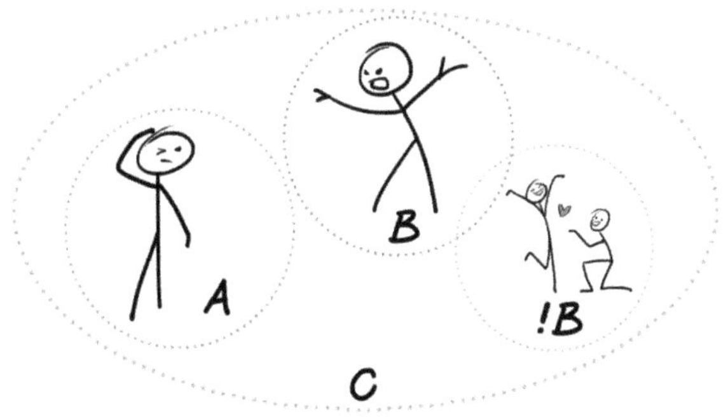

Crash and Burn

Client: *"I don't understand what is going on any more?"*

"We've had such a good life together, I wonder what the actual problem is?"

The boundary of C disintegrates in the presence of B and !B - those rules can no longer be true.

Stage 6 - Out of the Ashes

As we pass over into the sixth iteration, the edifice has collapsed, the structures that held the original issue together are no more - these fell away at Stage 5 - and **Out of the Ashes**, like a 'Phoenix', rises new knowledge and information.

Due to the fusion of B and !B the boundary structure of C must now be adjusted to allow for this global rearrangement, it is here new ideas and cognitions occur, this is Emergence E.

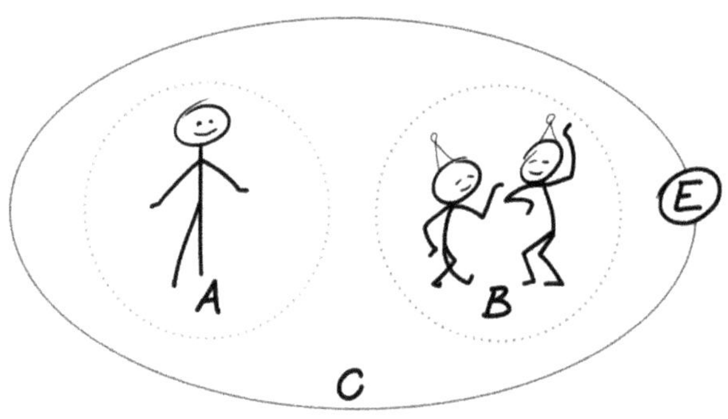

Out of the Ashes

Client: *"We always planned to be together forever. I know we can make this work, if we work together."*

"This is more about our love for each other and doing what makes us both happy!"

Stage 7 - The Pause

The **Pause** or moment to consolidate – this is the 7th or zero point. Here the client absorbs the learning from Stage 6.

Once consolidated, we can start again and begin a new set of processing on this new evolved information.

Everything comes back to A and is re-embodied.

The Pause and Consolidation

Client: *"I feel good about this now! There's still things to think about and plan, but I'm good."*

"Gawd, I do love that girl!"

Learning About Your Learning

This seven stage process is an epistemological exercise, one based on knowledge. As each stage is passed through, the client experiences another level of knowing about their issue.

As humans, we're generally unable to 'not know' something, so as soon as we have expressed our knowledge or our understanding of something, we become open to new knowledge and understanding developing about all that has preceded.

Thus, we have an unending, infinite flow of knowingness opening up before us, if we care to question what is there.

The summarised structure of this emergent flow discovered and proposed by David was as follows:

1. Proclaim
2. Explain
3. Reinforce and Expand
4. The Wobble
5. Crash and Burn
6. The Phoenixity - Out of the Ashes
7. The Pause

Over-Drive

This iteration of a simple question was given the term Over-Drive by David, it is possible that one may perform any of the following three Over-Drives:

- Over-Drive the client (A)
- Over-Drive the issue or current focus (B)
- Over-Drive the as yet uncharted space in and around A and B (C)

Some of the simplest questions to do this in these three categories are:

- A - What do you know?
- B - What does that know?
- C - What is between you and that?

These three sets can be further explored in more detail when utilising the Navigation techniques later. Gathering information from these external sources of B and C is of great benefit to the client, it is from these perspectives that we may more likely see new information enter in from D. In some ways A already knows what they know. It is the utilisation of these alternative viewpoints that help in bringing us new understandings.

It can be helpful to let the client know that, as well as verbally responding, they can also be representing their answers to the questions. This may be through writing down, drawing or any other way they wish to do it.

However, if a client wishes to, they do not have to verbalise anything during the session and they can just represent their answers. This is very useful if a client would like a content-free session. This is where a client may work with a therapist without ever telling them what the session is actually about, say for instance the material was embarrasing or just too difficult to talk about.

Check your Answers

Have a look through your answers from the exercise at the beginning of this chapter. Look to see if this emergent pattern is observable in your responses, note that in a short exercise like this the pattern may not be so visible, this is ok.

Are you able to locate 'The Reinforcement'?

Are you able to locate 'The Wobble'?

Are you able to locate 'The Phoenixity', the moment of Emergence?

3. Reinterpretation

The Download and Upload

The Pause or 7th stage is a key step in the EK process. It is here that the client has the opportunity to consolidate their system with respect to the information that has just emerged.

Once this has occurred the client is guided to a new Stage 1, where they review and gain a new interpretation of how things are for them now.

As the client is now restating their issue here, this is a new **Proclaim Stage**.

When clients are answering and writing down answers there are two parts to this stage:

1. Download
2. Upload

Download

The first is the Download step, where the facilitator asks the client:

"And, what do you know now?"

This can be seen metaphorically as a **download** from the clients mind or consciousness into a verbal form to share with the facilitator.

Upload

We then have the Upload step, where the facilitator instructs the client:

"Ok, now put all that on there"

indicating that the client should represent their answer on paper.

This may be thought of as an **uploading** process from the client to their paper.

Once the client has represented their answer on the paper, the client is usually directed to place this information (the paper) where it belongs in relationship to everything else (see Section 5. Navigation).

Notice that the client's understanding of their issue goes through at least two transformations to get onto the paper.

Representation as a Transformation

There are many forms in which our inner experience can be represented, the most recognised of these, as mentioned, is our verbal description.

A simple verbal transformation can be achieved by having the client sum up their understanding. Above, we have used David's *"And what do you know now?"* to aid in this. Another option could be:

- *"And how would you describe that now?"*

Any attempt of a transformation of our inner experience provides us with a new analysis of what we are experiencing. This reanalysis increases our understanding of our experience.

There is a simple law at work here, and that is:

To increase your understanding about something, connect with it.

Through the additional utilisation of writing, drawing, space and objects, we open up our mind to a multitude of concepts and constructs that are not readily available through language alone - along with this we have the ability to utilise distances, angles, directions, colour, shape, texture and form to bring even more depth to our awareness of what we are attending to.

This becomes a very rich experience for the client and offers multiple opportunities for their system to reinterpret their issue and their world.

Interestingly the word 'describe' comes from the *Latin describere, meaning de- 'down' + scribere 'write'*, literally 'to write down'.

4. Representation and Space

Writing about and Drawing the Inner Experience

This is done by having the client write or draw down their thoughts, feelings and experiences on paper, and then place these in the space around them, in relationship to themselves and previous papers or objects.

They can represent what is happening for them internally in whatever way they feel is appropriate; the availability for a varied use of colour, shape, language and symbols is recommended and encouraged.

In this manner, our inner worlds may be mapped externally by overlaying them into a room or a landscape. This has the useful effect of objectifying an internal phenomenon into a real geographic space, from which further information may be gained.

Materials

Using these techniques only requires a pen and paper, though the following may be acquired to allow you and your clients the maximum choice when expressing yourselves through writing, drawing and other creative expressions:

- A selection of pencils, crayons, coloured markers and pens
- A selection of paper sizes A3, A4 and A5
- Post It™ notes – various colours and sizes
- Flip / easel chart + paper
- Sellotape™ / Scotch Tape™ and Blue tak™ / Poster Putty™
- A selection of coloured wool or string

Objects

It has been observed that during sessions, clients can notice particular objects inside and outside the room which are 'perfect' representations of their ideas. Go with the client's flow and allow them to use these inferred significances as required. A client may also choose to utilise modelling clay to create a personal representation.

Space

The client can utilise all the space around them: the room, the windows, what is inside and outside, the table, floor, ceiling, walls - everything is available for placing or viewing the materials.

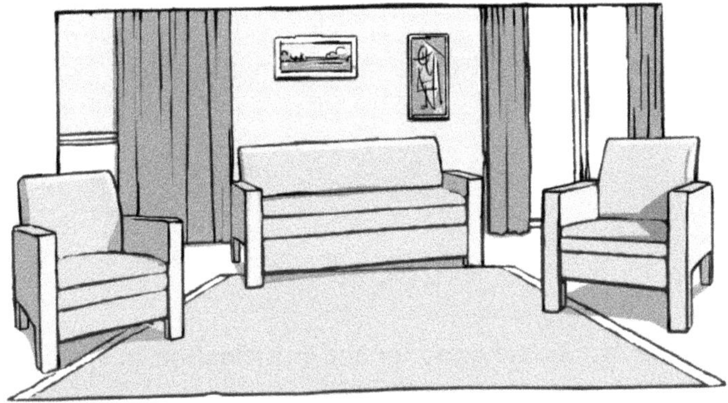

Be warned: you need to prepare yourself for sticky blue marks and sellotape marks spreading around your room and furniture! The use of Post It™ notes limits this.

If you are holding reservations about this happening, choose a different room to run your sessions in, as these reservations shouldn't be forced upon your client.

5. Navigation

The client's use of space is very personal and their use and interaction of it elicits the deeper structures of their issue.

To initiate this, have the client place their completed representation in space, by asking them,

"Okay, now place that where it belongs."

or

"Okay, and that belongs where?"

If there are already papers and information in the room, instruct,

"Okay, now place that where it belongs in relation to everything else."

or

"Okay, and in relation to everything else, that belongs where?"

For first time clients this can be a strange experience and they may be a little confused by this, as it may not be something they have ever considered or done before.

If the client has been given the time to figure out for themselves their spatial understanding and they are still having trouble you can begin to query if the paper 'should be close to them or far away?', 'should they be facing it or away from it?', 'should it be at the same level or above or below them?'.

In this way they will soon get to grips with what is happening for them and be able to place the paper where it needs to go. Later on, the client may change where the first few landed once they start to 'get in the groove'.

David created a full set of questions to kick-start a session off with, which he called *'The Clean Start'*; this process can elicit lots of information and requires training to deliver it correctly. For our purposes here, it is enough to have the client gain an understanding of their perceptual space. They will through further navigations, soon get into the flow.

If we relate this process of placing papers, representations of the clients ideas and considerations of their life, to the A-F Model we see that we are creating multiple B's.

Reference the Current Viewpoint

It is also possible to place representations of where A is when information comes from the 'Space of A', this is usually done by asking the client *'And what could this space be called?'*, the client then writes down the name and places it where they have been positioned. Later in the presented processes this will shown as 'Reference Viewpoint' or 'Reference the Space of A'.

Psychoactivity

Once a client has started placing their representations (papers) in the space around them, an interesting effect begins to occur. Through the placement of the papers the client will start to become aware of the developing relationships to the other papers, the surrounding space and themselves.

They have now started the process of literally mapping out their inner landscape. The moment they become aware of these developing relationships is when they and their landscape have become 'psychoactive'.

Just as the first explorers had no maps, neither do we and neither will the client. However, we do have a valuable set of intervention strategies to aid in this exploration and thus assist in this navigational and exploratory issue.

It is through the continued, iterative application of these strategies that solutions by the client may be found. These 'navigational' solutions are understood at a different level of thinking than the original problem was stated at.

Moving around a network of spaces, each representing aspects of the client and their life, offers the client multiple perspectives or viewpoints on their world. David gave the term **Meta-Drive** to the action of moving the position of the client (A) or the locations of the network information (B) - this aspect is detailed later.

More on the Over-Drive

Previously we looked at how the Over-Drive questions explored three areas in the client's ABC world. In this section as the client begins to move around their space, with multiple named spaces for A and potentially multiple B spaces, we can begin to have the client look at the relationships and bring these unique viewpoints into communication with each other.

For instance, we may ask the client *"And, what do you know about that from here?"* referencing their original statement.

Later though, as the clients spatial landscape begins to unfold, we could ask the same question about a previous space the client was in. Let us say the client had named a previous space "My Old Self" and the client was stood in a new position. We could ask some of the following questions:

- *"And what does 'My Old Self' know about where you are now?"*
- *"And what do you know about "My Old Self" now?"*
- *"And what does 'My Old Self' know about that (B)?"*

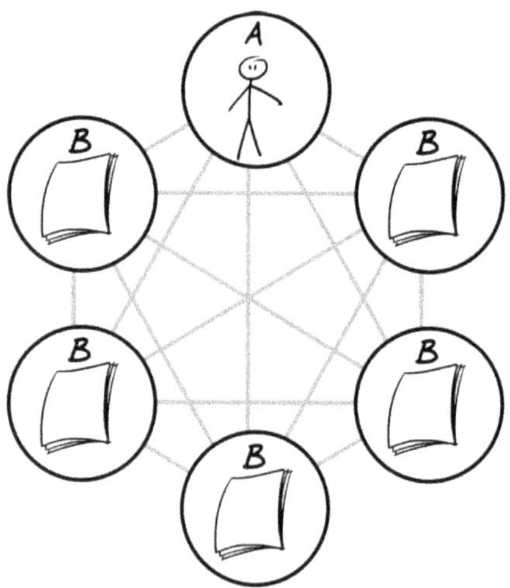

The Client Explores Each Node

As you can see through this technique we are able to create and explore any link between any two nodes in the developing network. This is useful for: checking in on how the client is doing, developing new sources of information or summing up what has occurred so far. A common technique is to have the client create six nodes in their network and then initiate the process of having each node explore every other node.

Once a client has moved away from a node (space), we can have them return to that space later and check in with what they know now in that space, it is here where we may begin to witness the evolution of the client's system in real time.

Clean Space

The use of 'Representation' and 'Space', along with 'Navigation', constitute the basic ideas of David Grove's Clean Space methodology.

See Appendix 1 for further resources on learning more about this very useful and powerful set of techniques.

Navigation of the client's inner world in this manner is a truly rewarding process; new information and new insights will nearly always emerge. To accomplish this navigation, the next ingredient to be added was the 'Algorithm'.

Clean Space Exercise

Follow the algorithm below to experience a basic Clean Space process:

1. On a piece of paper write down something that you'd like to work on or explore
2. Place that paper where it belongs
3. Position yourself in relationship to that paper
4. Ask, *"And, what do I know about that from here?"* (the original issue)
5. Write down your answer on a new piece of paper
6. Now, place the paper where it belongs in relationship to everything else
7. Ask, *"And, what could this space be called?"* (Spaces from steps #3 and #9)
8. Write down this name on a new paper and place it where you are
9. Move to a new space (you may also alter the direction you are facing)
10. Repeat Steps #4 to #9 five more times
11. Return to the original space
12. Ask, *"And from here, what do I know now?"*

This is presented as a self-facilitated process, it may be adapted to being facilitator led.

Personal Review of Clean Space Exercise

Write down your experience as the client:

____

____

____

Write down your experience as the facilitator:

____

____

____

And what do you know now?

____

____

____

6. Algorithms

The basic processes of Emergent Knowledge can be used in isolation when required in therapy and coaching, or they can be grouped together into specific algorithms to be run as integrated therapeutic processes.

This is one reason David gave each of the functions being performed a particular name:

Upload, Download, Over-Drive, Meta-Drive etc.

When using each of these functions integrated with the A-F Model opens us up to many choices and opportunities when developing algorithms.

Each algorithm may be given a full definition by providing a formula consisting of a set of basic processes. These formulas can be applied to any aspect of the client's ABC world, so questions can be asked of:

- the client (A)
- the issue (B), or
- anything else which the client is aware of (C)

The focus of the questions remain the same for a full round of six iterations. It is recommended to keep each round as simple as possible, enabling the client to add their own complexity.

For instance the simple Clean Space exercise from the previous section may be formulated as:

1. Create Mission Statement (B)
2. Meta-Drive A (run this section six times)
    a. Download from A
    b. Upload from A to new paper and place in space
    c. Reference Viewpoint A
    d. Move A to a new space
3. Download from original A Space - Reinterpretation from the original space

In this simple exercise we only asked one question from each space, later when asking questions in sets of six [+1] in each space, the client's language in each space may begin to reflect in a fractal/holographic nature the Iterative Pattern of Emergence.

This is a wonder to observe and is also a rock to hold onto, for when the client is in the 4th and/or 5th stages and is beginning to really 'heat up', as a traditional therapist we may of attempted to shift them out of the problem, but as an Emergent Knowledge facilitator we stay with the algorithm. Knowing that, as they continue to move on, their liberation awaits them in the 6th stage.

Key Principles

Some of the principles utilised in developing EK algorithms are:

- Locate and emerge existing and new viewpoints within the system
- Provide knowledge of the system from these viewpoints
- Determine relationships between the viewpoints
- Discover what exists in the spaces in between the viewpoints
- Balance of the system: grant equal value and significance to each viewpoint

New understanding occurs when the client sees their issue in a new light. This occurs in the present moment.

7. Present Time

Each of the questions and instructions given in EK processing are delivered in the present tense. We are looking to have the client access the required information in this moment.

You will recognise that the use of the word 'Now' is prominent, especially during the client's reinterpretation at the Proclaim (Recognition) stage, #1 in the Iterative Pattern of Emergence.

The client makes their changes in the here and now, so our intention is to bring the client to a moment in the here and now, where conditions are such that systemic change may occur for the client in a way that is congruent with the client's developing world-view in the current moment.

To enable this, it is considered in EK that the solutions to the client's problems have to come from the client. Anything that we as facilitators, or just as friendly advice-givers, attempt to add in, is likely to be dismissed or even opposed. To eliminate this, we work in a Clean manner with the client.

Role of the Facilitator and Client

In this chapter we look at the basic premises required for the facilitator and the client in Emergent Knowledge processing, finishing off with a look at how David was making his work 'Cleaner' with each new iteration.

The Facilitator

The facilitator does not make comment on, interpret for or lead the client. They only ask the questions or give the instructions as specified, then listen and acknowledge their response, until the client reaches the end of their process.

The facilitators acknowledgments are kept to a minimum, to avoid interruption. A simple, "Okay", "Yeah", "Uh-uh" will be sufficient to keep the session flowing.

EK processes are very simple and, once the client is familiar with the flow of the process, they may even begin to run it themselves. When this occurs, the client only requires active facilitator input when they halt or become lost in their space. This is usually recognised by the client bringing their attention back to the facilitator.

During the clients self-modelling moments, the facilitator simply becomes an observer of the system. This role could be known as the 'silent witness' position.

So, if your client is not looking at you, they are most likely still internally processing the last question or instruction you gave. Do not interrupt this.

In this silent witness position, one is to only observe and witness the client change. This is a highly privileged position, and the space you have been granted is to be given the utmost respect.

The Client

What is true for the client is true for the client, even if what they are stating appears to be clearly untrue and without reason to you as a facilitator; **it is true** for the client and you're not there to invalidate the client's understanding of their life.

If the client requests you may inform them of what Emergent Knowledge facilitation is, and what the process consists of, although even this is not a requirement, as they will very soon pick this up once they begin.

Can I Run These Processes on My Own?

Yes, this is possible, and it is intended that through practice you may achieve this.

Initially, though, it is recommended that you experience several facilitated sessions, especially if you have no direct experience of Clean Space or Emergent Knowledge.

It should also be noted that it is uncommon for a new *self-processing* client to fully connect with and directly experience the moments in which the process intends. The new self-processing client is generally operating from an intellectualised viewpoint when running EK processes alone.

This is mainly due to there being a split, where we have one aspect of the self presenting a part of the process to another listening aspect of the self, whilst that listening aspect is attempting to be fully immersed in the process at the same time!

Looking at the A to F Model, we are attempting to be at positions 'F' and 'A' in the same moment.

This can take a lot of time and practice to achieve, if at all for some people. Therefore, to begin with it's recommended that you find a companion to work with, and facilitate each other through these processes.

With the advent of EK, David was looking at how to

remove the facilitator from the process altogether - we discussed how this could happen many times. My current operational interpretation of how people may easily experience this is available at the Powers of Six website using an online facilitator see 'The Iterators I & II' once registered and logged into the website.

Here follows a short story on where I believe David first recognised how this could be done.

David's Prescriptions in New Zealand

Back when David was developing his ideas about Emergence and iteration, he ran an Emergent exercise in a New Zealand doctor's practice. As the clients were waiting for their appointment they were given the opportunity to see David.

The Client's Emergent Prescription

David would greet them and explain what he wanted them to do, he would ask them what they knew about their problem and then he would write down on his pad a series of questions. This he considered to be the client's 'Emergent Prescription'.

They would leave the room and write down their answers to his questions. Once complete, they were requested to come back and 'Download' to David on their experience.

This was a first descent into the realm of 'removing the facilitator from the process'. It was a success, and gave David the impetus to continue his research into more detailed and cleaner ideas and processes, which would become the core structure to his work in Emergent Knowledge.

Self-Modelling

The more one uses the processes presented here with a client, or on oneself, the easier and more fluid running them becomes. You and your client will become more proficient at recognising and interacting with the space around you. Especially when running the more advanced processes, such as Process #4 where you will find connecting to and experiencing prior and future moments, along with the ability to hold these in mind for comparison with your present state, becomes second nature.

This deeper understanding of our inner architecture and the relationship we have with it, is known as self-modelling. Once you become adept at this, the ability to self-process with EK develops rapidly.

On reading through the transcripts in this book you will see the moments where the client begins to self-model and takes control of their process.

Cleaner than Clean

It has been stated by David, myself and others that EK is 'Cleaner than Clean', or can be likened to Clean Language Mark 2.0. The reasoning for this is to be understood through several aspects:

First, is what David was looking to do above - 'Remove the facilitator from the process'. This is because the facilitator in Clean Language and Clean Space is introducing their own perception into the client's system by selecting and working with the spaces and the metaphors. Clean Space was a step away from Clean Language in this regard, but David was aware that the facilitator was still attached to the system.

Secondly, the questions utilised did not reference the client's system directly. The use of, *"What do you know about that?"* keeps the facilitator from getting directly involved; the client takes the questions where they need to go.

Thirdly, the Iterative Pattern of Emergence and EK model in general moved towards running algorithms, which are processes built to set structures. As David was developing therapeutic methods, he would reference his work as being in service to an aspect of it: in Clean Language, we were *"in service to the metaphor"*; in Clean Space, *"in service to the space"*; and finally, with emergence, *"in service to the algorithm."* As his aim was to 'remove the facilitator', the development of the algorithm was the key to this.

PRACTICAL I

- Process #1 - 'Emerging Moving'
- Process #2 - 'The Six Steps'

Process #1 - Emerging Moving

This process is an adapted version of Pam Saunders original from the Holigral training manual and her book, 'The Emperor's New Psychology'.

It can be run by a facilitator or by oneself. The purpose of this process is to orientate the client's attention to the present moment in time.

Introduction

If you run this on your own and find you have little change or effect, get someone else to ask you the questions. It has been noticed by some people that they can become 'intellectual' about the responses and look to calculate answers. Process #1 is experiential: feel it - just voice what is occurring in your thinking and your body as it is happening.

When you start, if you don't have a presenting issue to attend to, focus on a bodily sensation and follow the changes this goes through as the questions drive your system.

It is extremely simple and effective.

It works exceptionally well when you '**walk and talk**', so get up, move around and verbalise the answer to each question.

In fact, Pam states that "It is *ultra-important* to be walking, because the process is left-right footed."

And, now what is happening?

Client starts the session with an issue, desire or body sensation in mind to attend to.

Ask the client each question in turn, then continue to repeat steps 2 and 3, until the client expresses a positive shift in their well-being or presenting issue.

1. *"And, now what is happening?"*
2. *"And, as that is happening, now what happens?"*
3. *"And, as that happens, now what is happening?"*

Personal Review of Process #1

Write down your experience as the client:

____

____

____

Write down your experience as the facilitator:

____

____

____

And what do you know now?

____

____

____

An Analysis of Process #1

The iterative function of the two questions facilitates the client's system and enables change to occur. Their system begins to take on motion, so, where previously ideas or physical feelings were stuck, they now have an opportunity to flow again.

Once the system is in flow, the repeated questioning brings rhythm and pacing to the system, and the client begins to recognise they are existing in the moment of now, and their experience is an open flow.

This process is an absolute gem, the simplicity of it is a work of genius.

Given the time and attention, it can have great beneficial effects - be aware that this process may also require some additional skills and intervention to facilitate fully, this is where training and experience are key.

The included transcript shows how such a simple process can evolve into a multi-layered structure sometimes requiring some additional advanced techniques. This added complexity comes from the client and is acknowledged by the facilitator through these deviations.

Success may also be achieved in the use of this process as it is, without any additional devitation.

History of Process #1

This process was developed from Pam's understanding of the human mind, where one aspect is coded in fixed, locational thinking and another in fluid, momentum thinking. The two-question structures move between these.

- locational - "Now what happens?"
- momentum - "Now what is happening?"

This iterative transition between the two structures is designed to bring balance to both aspects and thus the client's presenting issue. Pam describes the original metaphor for the process as, 'to turn something static to something moving so that it could flow away, leaving a person in the now.'

Process #1 - Example Session (Carl)

Here I present a live session transcript of running Process #1. Carl came to me with a presenting issue that meant he had great difficulty in travelling, he had a fear of bridges whether walking across them or driving.

We visited a footbridge close by and ran the following session, I utilised the therapeutic technique of EFT (Emotional Freedom Technique) along with the EK question set, Carl tapped on a new EFT point for every question asked. You will see that I step outside of a strict adherence to the basic algorithm, this is due to several reasons:

1. The client began repeating some effects
2. To maintain a set of questions in line with the 8 EFT tapping points (so rounds are 7[+1] here)

To show this the transcript is shown in sets of Iterations. When I do step outside the algorithm, I utilise some of the original Clean Language questions to elicit more detail on aspects that are repeated by Carl.

We start the transcript as Carl and I, walk up to the bridge.

Live Transcript of Process #1

First Iteration

And now what is happening?

I'm becoming a bit apprehensive, slowing down a bit. Looking at it I'm thinking it's quite high. [Carl takes his first step onto the bridge]

I don't particularly like the look of it and the more I get out onto it, the more that feeling comes over me. [Carl steps back off the bridge]

My left leg is starting to go, my fists were both starting to clench, I was realising how high the bridge is and noticed the high sides of it. Theoretically I know I cannot fall over the sides, but my mind is saying "It's still not fully enclosed", it is worrying. I was starting to feel waves of worry and anxiety come over me.

And as that is happening, now what happens?

I'm starting to feel calmer about the whole situation, the state I was in wasn't doing me any favours.

And as that happens, now what is happening?

I still don't feel like getting close to it, and my left leg... it feels really quite tense.

And as that is happening, now what happens?

It still feels quite tense.

And as that happens, now what is happening?

I feel rigid in my entire body.

And as that is happening, now what happens?

My mouth has gone a bit dry.

And as that happens, now what is happening?

I can feel myself tapping under my arm, it's all changed to that.

What do you know now about all of this?

[Carl doesn't speak, he starts to walk out onto the bridge.]

Second Iteration

[There are no words for this iteration, as Carl walks out we simply move through the standard EFT points with no questions, he gets so far then physically clenches up and expresses a sound of discomfort, turns and walks rapidly off the bridge]

Third Iteration

And now what is happening?

I just wanted to get off it, it was almost as if I was getting to a point I couldn't physically walk, like something was stopping me.

And as that is happening, now what happens?

It's weird, because I got out there without any problem, and then like something instantaneously went 'Woomfph' and then a force field stop.

And as that happens, now what is happening?

My legs have gone all funny again.

And as that is happening, now what happens?

My left hand is clenching.

And as that happens, now what is happening?

It's starting to go through my head that I don't need to get across this bridge, so what's the point in even trying.

And as that is happening, now what happens?

I'm thinking, there's no way I can slip under this, I would have to do a massive jump to jump over the sides.

And as that happens, now what is happening?

I don't know what it is about it (the bridge), but I'm getting a real sense of worry about it.

What do you know now about all of this?

[Carl begins to walk back out across the bridge]

Fourth Iteration

And now what is happening?

It's in my legs, they are starting to feel heavy and also across here in my face.

And as that is happening, now what happens?

I've got dry lips and a dry mouth.

And as that happens, now what is happening?

Part of me is saying, "Why can't you just walk across the bridge, it's just a bridge it's like walking on a path. It's a path."

And as that is happening, now what happens?

I've got tension back in my leg, it's in both legs but in my left more than my right.

And as that happens, now what is happening?

I'm starting to feel tight.

And as that is happening, now what happens?

It's in my wrists.

And as that happens, now what is happening?

Oh! There's a wave coming over me.

[Carl rapidly walks back off the bridge.]

What do you know now about all of this?

[This question was missed as the 'wave' was investigated instead.]

Fifth Iteration

[Carl has now spoken of the 'wave' and 'Woomfph' several times and during the process he has also physically

represented it using his arms. I take this opportunity to investigate a little deeper with a Clean Language question.]

And where could that 'wave' come from?

It came from my mind, when I was looking at that (over the sides of the bridge). I established how far down it is from top to bottom and I thought "Oooo, it might not be safe".

And as that is happening, now what happens?

There's part of me that wants to start walking over that bridge, but then I visualise myself doing it and I get met by this force field that stops me.

And as that happens, now what is happening?

I feel almost rooted to the spot, as if it is trying to protect me.

And as that is happening, now what happens?

I'm scanning the bridge with my eyes. Scanning it, thinking "What is it, 40 yards to the other side?" So I'm having an internal argument of "Well, it's 40 yards, but you don't have to do it, so don't do it."

And as that happens, now what is happening?

I feel uncomfortable about this bridge. It's all over me, it's like half a centimeter all around. It's now filled with peace, that Ready Brek glow around me, it's as though the peace side of it was slightly more than the fear bit.

And as that is happening, now what happens?

I'm starting to feel lightheaded and sick. I don't feel like I'm going to be sick; but my tummy is going 'woah woah'.

And as that happens, now what is happening?

It feels so trivial, that guy has just come across it on a skateboard - and then there's this nervous energy.

And what do you know now about all of this?

That there is something stopping me from going across it and quite frankly that is ridiculous, because ultimately the bridge itself is perfectly safe, there are sides on it so you can't just accidently fall off the side and you can't slip and go underneath it. But there is something about it, and I just don't want to go across it.

Why is that? It's a bridge across a road, a little gorge. But I just feel there is no way I can go across it. I've walked out there a few times, but now I cannot even get on to the opening.

Sixth Iteration

And now what is happening?

I have these bizarre things, like if I'm in a meeting and my mind starts to drift I might get an impulse or a compulsion to go "What would happen if I punched that fella there?" Not in any way wanting to hurt that fella or even do it. My mind starts going through these scenarios because it's almost like an impulse or a compulsion and right now I'm looking at this and I'm thinking "Right, there's no way I'm going to jump over that bridge, but what would happen if I got to the middle and had an impulse or a compulsion to jump over the side of the bridge?"

And that's interesting as that has reminded me of walking across bridges, because I always put my mobile phone in my pocket, because if it was in my hand I could have the impulse to just throw it over the side.

It's a worry, that I am going to do something that I won't be able to control.

The situation itself, if you look at it from a risk assessment perspective, my Dad worked for the Health and Safety Executive (Carl laughs), it's pretty low-risk, without any outside external force it is completely no-risk. The only risk is if I couldn't control myself jumping over the side, and there is no reason I would jump over the side. So I should just be able to walk across it.

[Carl then begins to walk out onto the bridge, after a few steps he mutters 'ya ya ya']

[This next step is an advanced technique within the Emergent Knowledge methodology, it is based on the principle that the client's symptoms are unsuccessful attempts by the mind and body to heal itself. This next question is designed to encourage the symptom to further reveal itself. It's place within the current context may also begin to emerge.]

And what does that 'ya ya ya' know?

It's like this ridiculously strong force field, this fear and the start of something that will black me out or make me faint or do something that... it's the fear of losing control. That's what it is. Like the fear of having a panic attack. My hands feel clammy but dry..? This is weird, I've never had that before.

And whereabouts is that 'fear of losing control'?

It's like a huge thing pressing down on me, wanting to push me onto the floor. And I refuse to be pushed to the floor so I push back and then have to leave the situation.

And as that happens, now what is happening?

It's not there now.

[Carl walks back onto the bridge, he breathes heavily and emits a deep 'Whoooahhh', then turns and gets off the bridge]

I had to get off quick. That was the wave, that's the quickest it's ever come on, everything felt fine and then 'Shuu!', I had to turn around and come back. I was perfectly fine until then.

And as that is happening, now what happens?

I'm back to the stage of feeling uneasy about the situation, I get so far and then out of nowhere came that 'Woomfph' quicker and stronger than ever before, but I got out that far with no worry at all.

[Carl's system is now presenting this 'Woomfph' (and 'wave') on a regular occurrence, I deviate from Process #1 to elicit

where Carl has experienced this before. This question is from my own developments in EK.]

And that 'Woomfph', when have you had that before?

When driving.

And before that?

When I was a really young boy riding my bike, my dad had come to pick me up from a friend's house. And I wanted to go my own way which was probably twice the distance, and my dad got fed up and said "I'm going this way Carl and you're coming with me."

I was only 6 or 7 and I decided I was going the other way, my dad called my bluff and walked off. I thought he would come with me, he's my dad he has to. And as I was going my way, this car pulled up on the other side of the road.

It was that time at school when you had to watch stuff about 'stranger danger', I remember that this car pulls up on the other side of the road, I start panicking and then that 'Woomfph' as I am standing with my bike and then having no memory until I remember my dad is stood next to me saying "Come on! Let's just go this way."

Then I felt totally comfortable, with the calmness there. It was a red and blue bike, there's a laurel hedge. That feeling of fear, of utter panic and terror made me black out until my dad was there.

And is there anything else?

I probably made up a lot more of that than there actually was, when it probably wasn't true. It just happened to be when we'd watched a class video on the Friday and at the weekend I decided to go 'this way' instead of 'that way' and this car pulls up totally coincidently and because my dad had gone off and I was on my own I felt vulnerable and I had this 'Voom' (The 'Woomfph') of fear and panic - my throat's gone quite dry now (coughs, then yawns) - Oh I'm sorry I feel so very tired.

And where could that 'tired' come from?

That's from the adrenaline, why I feel so sleepy.

Seventh Iteration

And now what is happening?

A dry mouth, I feel like I've just gone through something there.

I've occasionally thought about that memory from time to time, but when it came up there, I thought "Why? That's not relevant". But it is, it's massively relevant - it's as though I have that memory everyday, but I don't. I can't actually remember the last time I had that memory.

What do you know now about this?

This bridge and walking across it, it's not that; something about that triggers something.

[Carl starts to walk onto the bridge, has a reaction and walks back off]

What I am experiencing in relation to that bridge is not relative.

And experiencing, and what has happened to the 'Voom'?

It wasn't as intense, it softened the "Stop you're not going any further".

[Carl walks back onto the bridge]

And now what is happening?

I want to get lower because I am feeling exposed. Whoa, yes it is feeling exposed.

[Carl rapidly walks off the bridge]

It's lack of protection, feeling exposed and the situation is out of my control. I can see how all those three link back to this situation with me and my bike and my dad and the car pulling up.

And there is a difference now, when I'm a boy I am feeling exposed, I am there on my own, I don't have the protection of my dad, which when I am a young boy I certainly feel my dad offers me massive amounts of protection. And the situation feels like it is not in my control. Because I have lost some minutes of it.

[Carl begins stretching and rubbing his left leg]

[As run previously with the 'Woomfph', I query the repeating symptom of Carl's left leg.]

And what does that leg (indicating towards Carl's left leg) know?

It was there, it experienced it... I got on my bike... I got on my bike and pedalled like mad... I got on my bike and pedalled like mad... My dad **didn't** meet me in the same place, I got on my bike and pedalled like mad.

... What happened? ...

I was at my friend's house number 3, my dad came and picked me up, I was on my bike, dad went that way, I went this way and had to pedal like mad because my dad had called my bluff he wasn't following me - "Oh shit! I'm on my own here, I know which way I'm going" So I pedalled and I got to the end of the road and then the car pulled up, someone wound the window down and started talking to me.

It was a white car, a Ford Escort. Shortly after that my dad turned up, he'd gone another way which was quicker to come and meet me and teach me a lesson - which he certainly did - I was relieved to see my dad and then we went home. He spoke to the people in the car, they probably knew us and were saying "What are you doing out here on your own?"

So when I set off on my own, at that point where I felt the danger I'd already pedalled at that point and stopped to speak to the person in the car.

And is there anything else?

This is just little Carl's leg that has been pedalling, pedalling really fast.

[Carl is gripping and releasing his hands]

And is there anything else about 'clammy hands'?

From gripping the bike, from pedalling the bike and using the brakes to stop the bike and speak to the person in the car.

[Carl starts to walk on the bridge getting further than before, then stops and moves back]

I can start to feel it.

And feel it, is that the same or different than before?

It's softer, it doesn't come on as strong. [Carl goes back to the bridge]

And as that happens, now what is happening?

Right now if I just concentrate on the floor put my head down and don't look around. I'm slow. I'm struggling to move my feet forwards. I'm starting to feel dizzy now.

And as that is happening, now what happens?

I just want to get off the bridge, I feel dizzy. [Carl walks back off the bridge]

The dizzy has gone, I've started to process things in my mind, I feel as though every time we are getting further, before something happens and the effect of it is slower to come on. It eventually reaches a similiar intensity.

It's almost like I can start to process it now, but it's taking up an awful lot of my resources to do that. [Carl walks back out on to the bridge, we get close to halfway across which is the furthest we have been so far]

And as that happens, now what is happening?

I'm looking up at that bedroom window and wondering if there is anyone in that house thinking "What the hell are they doing?"

Right, I feel as though I need to hold you. [Carl grabs my arm]

We are over halfway now and there is no turning back, I'm nearly there... I'm on the other side. [Carl breathes out a big breath]

And as that is happening, now what happens?

I did that, I came across there - my eyes were open, but I almost stopped seeing, I just kind of blurred everything so I couldn't actually see anything. Before I was holding onto the railing and I was looking around trying to rationalise everything, then I was looking just at the floor, I did look up to the right at the window. I wasn't massively focused on seeing anything, just "I'm going to get to the other side"

I held onto your upper arm, then we were past halfway and I started looking at the path again, and it became the path. Then I focused on this bit here, I thought it looked like the massive footprint of a bird, I thought "I'll head for that."

I didn't get the 'Voom', there was a slow build up but I could control it more, that culminated in grabbing your jacket. My leg is pretty still now, I can't remember if my leg did anything out there, my attention had moved onto what I was seeing, which is interesting because I usually feel, I'm very kinaesthetic.

[This is an interesting comment as Carl's attention has now moved from a predominantly internal focus to an external focus. This shift in perspective may be enough for a resolution to occur.]

And what do you know now from this side?

From this angle it looks scary, [Carl moves] and from here it doesn't look that scary.

And what kind of scary is that scary?

The kind if something was going to go wrong it would. It's the angle, from here the railings don't look very high, you can see the perspective more.

Phwoar! I feel like I've done a lot of stuff here. [Carl rests against a wall] Jesus! My legs feel like I've done 100 squats or something, like a massive leg session in the gym. How weird is that?

And is there anything else?

That memory is the first time I can remember being scared. Outside the bubble of parents and being looked after, of being really, really scared - that's the first time. The first time I felt real fear and being scared, there's definitely something connected to that and it's where I've learned the response to it.

Is that a good place to finish the session?

Yes it is, we may as well go this way, we've done it once. Let us see what happens... [Carl walks over the bridge without grabbing me]

Carl's Feedback

After a week I catch up with Carl to check in on how things are going:

"It's clear I've been processing a lot. The journey home after the session was fine. I was extremely tired so went the back roads by choice as I didn't want to undo any of the good work of the session. I wondered if this was avoidance but the thought of driving home on the major roads and across bridges didn't make me feel anxious as usual so I believe this was a sensible choice."

He continues, "Similarly since, I have no anxiety thinking of journeys that involve big roads or across bridges, but haven't needed to do one yet. I think I'll deliberately set out at the weekend to drive a route that involves a bridge as well as try some walking routes. Will report back!"

I ask Carl how this experience is different from before the session. He replies "It's a big improvement as over the last 18 months, I've had symptoms of anxiety (similar to those in the session) when simply contemplating journeys!" I catch up a few weeks later and he updates me with, "I don't get anxious anymore."

Many thanks to Carl for giving his permission in sharing this. Note that all names and references have been changed.

Process #2 - The Six Steps

Here follows one of the basic Emergent Knowledge processes David created. It clearly presents four of the core functions of EK:

- Download
- Upload
- Over-Drive
- Meta-Drive

Introduction

The process is written as though being delivered by a facilitator, though it is entirely possible to adapt it and use this process for self-facilitation.

Through the process the client moves through six separate spaces and in each one of these spaces a series of iterative questions are asked of them about what they know about their 'issue'.

Each space they occupy is appropriately named and labelled thus providing a visual and spatial marker to represent the evolving knowledge and the system in which it belongs.

The Six Steps Process

1. Download and Upload from A
    a. "What would you like to work on / attend to this session?"
    b. "Put all that on there" - client writes down their answer
2. Locate B
    a. "Place that where it belongs" - client places paper
3. Meta-Drive A
    a. "Position yourself where are you now in relation to that." - client moves to a space
4. Over-Drive A
    a. "And what (else) do you know about that from here?" ask this six times
        i. Note that clients often write down these answers, this information could be placed at A, B or even somewhere new.
5. Reference Viewpoint of A
    a. "And what could this space be called?" - client writes name of space
    b. "Place that where it belongs"
6. Download and Upload from A
    a. "And what do you know now about all of this?"

b. "Represent that" or "Write that down"
c. "Place that where it belongs"

7. Meta-Drive A
    a. "Move to a new space"
8. Repeat Steps 4. to 7. five more times
9. Meta-Drive A
    a. "Return to your original space"
10. Download from A
    a. "And what do you know now from here?"
11. Recognise Difference
    a. "And what is the difference between what you know now and when you started?"

Personal Review of Process #2

Write down your experience as the client:

____

____

____

Write down your experience as the facilitator:

____

____

____

And what do you know now?

____

____

____

Process #2 - Example Session (Sam)

Here follows a full session transcript from a client running through the Six Steps process - note that I made a few detours from the standard algorithm during this process as information being presented from Sam had been given enough significance to initiate this.

Sam also makes her own changes and emergent developments throughout the process, these are recognised and referenced as they occur. This is a common phenomenon as a client begins to access and work within their psychoactive landscape - as a facilitator we simply acknowledge the emergence and continue with the algorithm.

Also for the observant among you, you may notice that I only run the Over-Drive section using sets of five, not six as defined - this is an error on my behalf as I was utilising the 'Name this Space' step as the final 'Rest and Consolidation' stage - however, a successful result was still achieved.

Many thanks to Sam for giving her permission in sharing this. Note that all names and references have been changed.

Live Transcript of Process #2

First Iteration

What would you like to work on?

My father's dementia, and mother's resistance to help - her fierce independance, depression, shutting down. Being contrary. [This is referenced as 'B' in this transcript]

Ok, place that where it belongs.

I don't want any of it at the moment, so I want it as far away as possible, but it is actually there. [Sam indicates directly in front of her face]

It is presenting itself, right here now.

Ok, so place yourself where you are now in relationship to that

I'm right here, in the middle.

[Sam stands in front of the paper on the flipchart and puts her face against it]

And what do you know about that from here?

That I'm stressed with it all, I'm overwhelmed and it's too much for me. It's all weighing on me. I feel regressed back to age 8/9.

And what else do you know?

I don't have to tolerate some of her attitude anymore. I can stand back from it and be my independent self; but I need to be, I want to be, there for her but more for my father. They're both suffering.

And what else do you know?

The way I'm dealing with it at the moment is like I have all of this stuff in a different box, it's all emotions - but I'm keeping a lid on all of it, because I have to for my father's sake. I'm keeping it all in [mental] boxes.

[I make a slight detour from the process here, as while Sam is talking about the boxes she is gesturing to her left and right, up and down - this prompts me to have Sam locate this sensory information.]

And where are boxes?

They're all over, these ones here are ok with lids on, but these ones have their lids open.

And what else do you know?

There's a distance thing as well, I live here and they live in Aberdeen. They're happy, but it's all starting to break down, it's reaching crisis point.

And what else do you know?

It's hugely emotional and it takes me back to when I was younger and I had to deal with my mother's absence. She would have to leave every 4/5 years and go to America which my father didn't know about, and then she would come back and they would get back together. I learnt to cope with it, my brother didn't and he hasn't seen them or me for over 10 years.

[Another detour, I have Sam represent a younger her and younger brother these are placed in relationship to the information already there, more information now emerges.]

I can see that everything is just like it was back then, I am the carer now and I was the carer back then - and all the emotion is all part of back then. It's like I'm going through it all again, but in a different situation. Mum has an 'Iron Will' that has always been there, it's all encompassing.

And what could this space be called?

Disempowering, regressed, angry, crushed mentally - it all sounds so negative, but it's not, she's fantastic company. There was a lot of happy times, laughter and a house of love. {Space #1 - Proclaim}

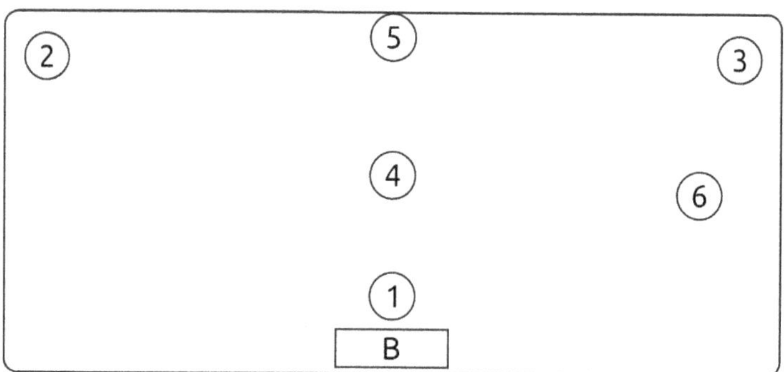

Sam's Six Spaces

[The image above shows all six spaces Sam visits on her journey, use this as a reference in this transcript.]

Second Iteration

What do you know now about all of this?

It's massive and a lot of high expressed emotion and it's just like a Pandora's box open and there is so much to deal with, but I can only do so much - Looking at it now, seeing how much is there. It's massive. I have to keep a lid on the box or it will overwhelm me.

Find a new space.

[Sam takes several steps back from her original statement]

I'm here, I've got more perspective on it now - having this distance is good, as I am relieved from it all. The real distance is good and this distance is good, I don't have to deal with it all at once. There's guilt here but not a lot.

And what do you know from here about that?

Maybe I could do more - I thought it was guilt, but it's not - it's a great sadness for my dad - I couldn't spend time with my dad because my mother is so controlling.

And what else do you know?

[Sam continues to step further back into the corner of the room]

Ultimately I am in charge of it all - but life happens, then hearing a song or seeing a greeting card and that can take me right back to there.

And what else do you know?

It's a very sad situation, but it was going to happen, their decline - I didn't really think about it. Professionally I know about this, but when it is your own parents it is different.

And what else do you know?

I need some support, as it is mentally draining and exhausting, especially the frustration that I want to help but she won't let me.

And what else do you know?

Here I'm more in charge.

And what could this space be called?

It's my self-preservation space, it has to be protected. {Space #2 - Explain}

Third Iteration

What do you know now about all of this?

I'm in charge - I have to stay here to deal with any of that {'B'}. This will always be my safe place, my constant. I've got to keep bringing myself back to here, especially when I get overwhelmed with the sadness over there {Space #1}. I need to accept help from others.

Find a new space.

[Sam moves to the adjacent corner of the room] {Space #3 - Reinforce and Expand}

And what do you know from here?

Physically and mentally this gives me another perspective. Here feels like me seeking support from others and making sure I do that. It's a reminder that I need to accept support from others. But also accept the limitations that I cannot deal with it all, some of it is going to happen regardless of what I say or do.

And what else do you know?

That it's ok to let go of the responsibility. Though when the 'Tide of Life' is happening, the vulnerability could easily knock me off center - so I need to be over there {Space #2} and over here {Space #3}.

[*The emergence of the 'Tide of Life', is a clear indication of psychoactivity within Sam's landscape - this is then followed up by her referencing prior spaces and linking them all up to one another, we are witnessing a natural Navigation interaction. As Sam progresses, the 'Tide of Life' and the resulting emerging landscape from this becomes significant.*]

And what else do you know?

[Sam moves to a new space in the centre of the room and states that this is where she is now - we continue from this space] {Space #4 -The Wobble}

It's like I'm in the ocean, wading through all of this - the tide is going to come in and I need to get to my safe space {Space #2}, if I don't get there then that's me drowning. Wading in, going very carefully, always navigating and that's exactly how I feel just now - with my Mum and Dad's situation, my own family situation, my work situation, I'm on 'hyper-vigilance' - but I always get back to the lighthouse back here.

[*New aspects keep coming up for Sam such as the 'lighthouse', this is a result of the client's interaction with, and therefore the increasing awareness of, their landscape. It is also interesting to see how this emerging metaphor has a holistic scope to it, this is no longer just about a singular issue.*]

And what else do you know?

I feel very strong, but I also feel very exhausted - because it's constant, it's tiring, I've got to make sure I get some rest and respite. The respite is these two islands {Spaces #2 and #3}."

And what else do you know?

I can see it all, the sand, the waves, very strongly I can see it.

And what could this space be called?

Drowning and Hyper-Vigilance {Space #4}

Fourth Iteration

What do you know now about all of this?

I'm either here {Space #2} or there {Space #3} and I'm very much in charge and the sand here is firm, it's solid and it has to stay that way. I've got to stay here and there, and there will be times when life becomes difficult and the sands will shift.

[with no prompting Sam now begins to draw out her landscape on a piece of paper]

If that's the situation and that's the waves, then here's the islands and that's the causeway - and I've just realised that this is actually a beach - I've just made that connection! This bit's good.

[Sam now places the picture in between her two islands and begins to walk between them, along the beach]

I can actually walk from here to here and I'm safe the tide can come in but it can't come further than the beach. I've got more beach and island than waves and that is good! It's very liberating, it just went 'click' and I've got more strength over this than I realised.

[As a new space has just emerged, this is referenced]

And what could this space be called?

Sam's Beach {Space #5 - Crash and Burn}

And what do you know from here?

I know that this is like in the middle of it all and I'm still wading through it but I also know there is a big wave that could keep hitting me and overwhelming me. And I can't stop the wave but what I can do is keep going to this place. And for more resilience and for support and for distance and perspective. I can also just walk on the beach and take my time until I'm ready to deal with that. Accept friends and support and look at it and just stay on the beach and on the solid sand until I'm ready to swim out again and deal with some more of it, but this has to stay solid. And that out there is the drowning point, the danger zone, that's like a rip tide. Hmmm, a 'Rest in Peace' tide.

And what else do you know?

It's good, I see it clearly that is I just can't go here {Space #4}. I can't go here unless I'm fully mentally prepared or even if I do go there I have to be aware that rather than let it all absorb me. I have to exercise vigilance. This is carrying me downstream, I need to go back and I need to draw on my own reserve and only go back when I feel ready to deal with it and that's only going to happen if I stay on that island, that island and on the beach where I can get a better perspective of it all, and just regain strength to go back into it.

And what else do you know?

Well I know so much more now because of my age, because of life experience, far more knowledgeable now and able to stand on the beach and stay safe. Whereas at 8 and 9 I was in the middle of all this and drowning and encompassed by it, that was not a good place to be.

And what else do you know?

Well, now he *[Sam's Brother]* has made his beach and islands stronger, possibly before I did. I think he's been on his beach and islands for awhile. But at 5 and 6, he was the same as me. I was here and he was just holding my hand trusting me, and I had to get him to islands or a beach which were grandparents or dad at the time, so I was always helping him to get there but I do feel, because he hasn't been communicating with me for 10 years, I do feel that he stood back a long time ago with his family. He made his beach and his islands and decided to never go there, he's never gone there. Because he's never been to see them. He's just not going in the water, fullstop.

And what else do you know?

That it's all manageable as long as I stay on solid ground and keep accessing support and look after myself and only go there when I really need to but also when I am here be aware of the state of hyper-vigilance and exhaustion this causes me, that it's just not possible to maintain that state consistently. So give myself that break, allow myself to go here, here and here. Whereas. I was never allowed that when I was 8/9 it was all just cope or not cope with whatever happened, I was never allowed that choice. I had to go with what was going on, but now I'm allowed that and I can take control back.

Fifth Iteration

What do you know now about all of this?

That I am in charge of all this and it's ok, I just have to keep doing what I'm doing. Because from here, on the islands and the beach I am in a far better place mentally and physically to lay all the boxes out, put the lids on them, and when I am ready to take a lid off one at a time and deal with that.

Find a new space.

[Sam starts walking around with her eyes fixed on the original statements]

I feel I have to keep seeing that.

[Sam finds a space a few steps out from Space #3] {Space #6 - Out of the Ashes}

And what do you know from here?

Leave all that and just concentrate on completely different things, fun and escapism, as that's vital to re-energize me; that's so vital and important for my self care. But that also re-generates me to then pull back to here {Space #6} and here {Space #5}.

And what else do you know?

This is as vital if not more so than the self care aspect because without it I become unwell, stressed and would be unable to deal with this situation or situations, so this is a part of me to keep in perspective by having other things, like happiness, sleep, enjoying the feeling of now being attached to this. To take my time.

And what else do you know?

That this brings the strength to go back in the boxes or, it's also ok to not open the boxes for a while. My box of self care has got to be full and strong and solid. And I need to indulge in that a bit and not feel that I have to go here until I'm really ready because the more perspective I get here, the stronger I will be there. But bearing in mind that it will be overwhelming.

I feel so distant from it *[the original issue]*, it's really good, from the first question I definitely feel the difference.

And what else do you know?

That it's ok, it has to be done and it will be done and it's okay to be done but not just for me, for my son and daughter to see that this is how it's better to cope, because you have to care for yourself first. To kind of perpetuate your strength. But it's okay to do this and don't feel guilty, don't feel guilty about that. Whereas I feel guilty is over there {Space #1} because it was always about my mother and what she needed whereas this is okay not to feel guilty - in self care.

And what else do you know?

That's about it to be honest like the self care is the paramount thing. I can't really think of anything else...

I mean, another tangent is the box that is my brother. There's a huge emotional minefield. I'm not going near that at the moment because it's resurged a lot of feelings for me about how I'm guilty by association, he hasn't talked to me in 10 years and he hasn't been near my mum and dad even though he lives a couple of streets away.

It feels like it is my responsibility or incumbent upon me, I want to write to him saying 'Mum and Dad are unwell, you need to visit soon. I just feel you should know.' But, I'm not opening that box yet.

So I feel empowered here. A lot of empowerment comes from here.

The empowerment is there but guilt's a funny thing, you don't realise you're feeling guilty, but you kind of think: "Limit it or I will be back to that. I should be doing it, but no no, just you stay here a bit it's okay because you'll gain more strength from here than anywhere else."

And then you can go back to that in your own time and your own choice. And there's far less pressure here, but that pressure can sometimes... It's kind of like it's because it's always been within you because when you were younger there was that pressure, like an unspoken pressure. You don't realise, you just don't realise that it's there, but it takes you back to the situation where you need to be the one that's helping and doing and fixing. You need to be back fixing. I shouldn't feel guilt or feel more pressure.

Here is not to feel guilty or not to feel pressure.

And what could this space be called?

Well, it's the best space - a vital space to reinforce the fact that it's necessary, it's almost like I don't have to justify it. {Space #6}

Sixth Iteration

[I recognise that Sam has already created extra spaces for herself during the process, thus giving her six perspectives. As well as the emergence of her 'Empowered' space. So I began to close the session, first though I check in with a few of the nodes created during the process.]

What's in between The Best Space {Space #6} and The Beach {Space #5}?

I'm standing a lot in the way of myself with that. But I need to make that time, that time is reflective time. I need to prioritise that. Also, if I start opening boxes before I'm ready to do that. Because that age-old, ingrained sense of pressure will always resurface, so I've got to not let that happen. So not to stand in my own way.

What do you know from here about Hyper-Vigilance {Space #4}?

I'm acutely aware of how exhausting, draining and disempowering that is, so to get away from that, swim back to here.

Return to the First Space

And what do you know from here now?

I don't feel nearly as overwhelmed with that, I was really in the middle of all of that. But I feel so much stronger now, I feel like I've got a bigger box to put it in and the lid is on tighter.

It was all so busy in my head, always there despite what you're doing - Now I feel so much more in control, I feel I've visibly made a stronger beach, this island, I've reinforced this island - the beach is solid here. This island is strong - but I still feel like I'm a coast guard always checking - but most importantly is being able to switch off from being the coastguard and being hyper-vigilant and take some time out - and it's ok, the tide isn't going to come in suddenly and sweep everything away, it's alright, it will still be there.

You need to shut down a bit, do self care and reflection time, meditation, and be in that space for yourself, your self-preservation, somebody else will be looking after the beach and the islands.

And where would you like to be to finish off?

I am here [Sam moves back to the Best Space {Space #6}] and I'm going to stay here for a while and feel joy and freedom and happiness - yeah I'm definitely here - this is what happens now.

I'm going to draw all this out. This picture will stay with me, that's a picture for life, it's great!

Sam's Feedback

Three days later, Sam contacts me:

Hi Matthew, just to say a massive thank you for your time on Monday. I found the whole session extremely helpful and liberating! I literally feel much lighter mentally for what you drew out verbally and physically. Wonderfully cathartic and therapeutic, intense as it was at times! I also appreciate having the paperwork from the session to review when I feel is the right time. At the moment it's in its tightly sealed box as I am about to book a holiday for Steve and I on a firm sunny beach! Take Care

THEORY II

We are now crossing a bridge from David's legacy over to my own emerging developments, which leads us to a working model and definition for personal Inner Peace.

- Redefining the Iterative Pattern
- Defining the Eternal Moment of Now

Redefining the Iterative Pattern

This chapter provides a deeper analysis of the Iterative Pattern of Emergence, also known as The Power of Six. We take a revised look at what the pattern is, its structure and also review this with client transcripts.

The Pattern Revised

I have observed and utilised the 'Iterative Pattern of Emergence' countless times since being introduced to this by David in 2007. The pattern came from David's understanding at the time and it was still a work in progress. Once the pattern was recognised, it was observed, and proposed that we were all subject to this pattern. In this way, it has been considered that the pattern is mystical or spiritual in nature - including myself at times.

So I have researched many avenues to gain some deeper understanding and comprehension as to why this would be so, especially with so many cultures experiencing the same patterning.

I have come to the conclusion that the pattern is as it is, not because of some ancient imprint (although Pam Saunders has spotted there is a very interesting and conspicuous link to the seven days of the week - this is detailed in Appendix 2), but simply because this is the structure and nature of our awareness expanding. Each stage logically proceeds from the one preceding it; once a stage is reached you cannot backtrack to now not knowing! Therefore, there is only going forward and, ultimately, passing through this pattern.

Taking the logical approach, the expression of this pattern is validated as we look at how one's awareness naturally expands:

- Once one becomes aware of something, we are then open to recognising more aspects and then how these aspects inter-relate.
- One is now at the point where one may become aware of those aspects that are not immediately associated, but which also run contra to the aspects already unveiled.
- At this point a re-analysis is required to discover how all these concepts can exist at once. To achieve this, a revision of the current set of rules and boundaries is required, and this begins with the deconstruction of the existing structure.
- Now a new set of rules and boundaries may be developed which can envelope all that is now observed and known about.

The basic elements of this pattern may be observed in the Hegelian Dialectic.

Where there are three dialectical stages of development:

1. A thesis (Stages 1-3)
2. An anti-thesis (Stage 4: The Wobble) which contradicts the thesis
3. The synthesis (Stages 5 & 6) which is the result of the reconciliation of these two

All of which drives towards a new understanding, which we now call Emergence. This process may continue indefinitely, see overleaf.

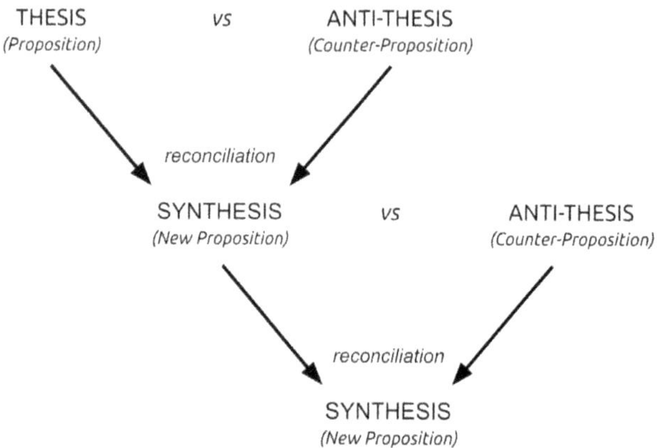

Hegelian Dialectic

We may also observe it within the scientific method:

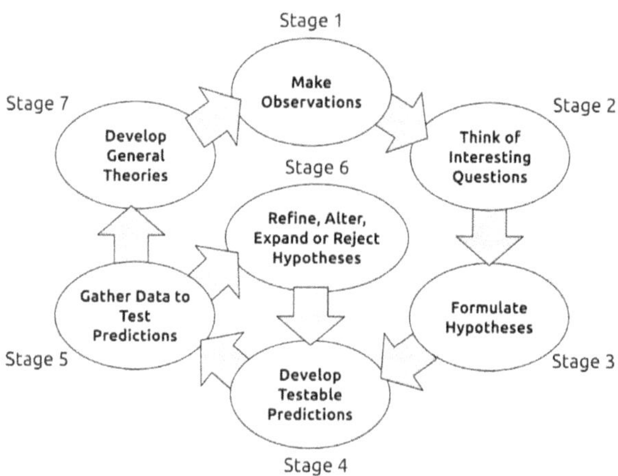

The Scientific Method as an Ongoing Process

The Seven Stages of Emergence

This new understanding has led me to review the pattern and offer an updated set of constructs. Note that the underlying structure remains the same.

1 - *Recognition*: We begin with the client *recognising* and making an initial statement about their issue - This is the first stage, we now accept this stage to be synonymous with David's beginning stage where he has the client write up on paper what it is they would like to work on.

2 - *Effect*: In the second stage, the client provides us with an explanation of what is happening and perhaps how this issue is *effecting* them.

3 - *System and Form*: Moving on from these effects, the client begins their exploration of how this occurs. What is the operation of the world in which they operate? What is the *system*? It is here that the client will provide us with the boundary conditions - that which defines the *form*. It is here where we will be introduced to the rules, ultimatums and required conditions.

4 - *Consequences and Contradictions*: As the client progresses, they push forward and offer up what happens as a result of this system, these are the *consequences*. The facilitator now waits... for the client may spend a little time here before offering *contradictory* information, maybe mentioning what it is like when the problem isn't there or what it was like in the past before they had this problem.

5 - *Unravel*: Once the client has stated this contradictory information, then observed this in relationship to the consequences and the information from the first four stages, it becomes apparent that the original form and structure of the client's system is now no longer valid. This then must start to *unravel*. After this has occurred, the information leftover has the opportunity to come together. This we call the unification and is part of the next stage.

6 - *Emergence*: On coming to this point of a unification, the client's system re-evaluates, the result of which then appears in consciousness. Usually surprising the client - the new rules and boundary conditions that evolve here are what we call *Emergence*. This effect provides a reference to how we cannot go back to 'the way things were' for that time has now passed. We may only recover from and learn to live in acceptance, experiencing a new world that encompasses our whole time track, in a holistic manner, thus the final stage.

7 - *Rest and Consolidation*: Now that the client has a new world-view, they reflect on it and how it all relates back to themselves. This is just like in David's original patterning: it is a stage of *rest* where there is a *consolidation* of the new information and the client.

A Client's Process

To aid in sharing this updated patterning with you, I will use a client's responses from their self managed process from the online Iterator at http://www.powersofsix.com.

In order to do this each of the client's responses are presented at list position (a.), along with a short description of how this response relates to that stage in the process below it at list position (b.)

The process being run was the "Full Six Steps" process devised by David and implemented into the Iterator by myself.

Our client, who we'll call Walter, starts their process writing down what they'd like to work on and is then iteratively asked,

"And, what (else) do you know about that?"

1. *Recognition* - validating 'B' exists
   a. Weight-Money-Work. Why is being at a healthy weight a lifelong struggle? Why does it always feel that having enough money is a struggle? Why do I tend to dislike the work I do?
   b. Here's the first statement - Walter is beginning his process and exposes that which has been holding his attention. His questions and personal responses are simply stated as he currently understands them. The problem is *Recognised.*

2. *Effect* - validating the relationship between 'A' and 'B'
    a. Weight, money and work are three areas that I am most unhappy about in my life.
    b. Walter's statement that *'..I am most unhappy about..'*, is representative of showing what happens to Walter with respect to his issue at Stage 1 - very much an *Effect.*
3. *System & Form* - looking at the structure of the world of 'A' and 'B' which is 'C'
    a. They seem to be interconnected - I eat too much when I am stressed about money or work. My work does not generate enough money. I do not have enough money to do the things that I would like.
    b. Walter is starting to look at the structure of his issue and himself. The idea of the *'seem to be interconnected'* tends towards us considering that Walter is now beginning to look at his issue as a *system.* See how the separate aspects of the system are now affecting the others.
4. *Consequences & Contradictions* - the repercussions and also the inverse of 'B' in 'D' = '!B'
    a. I am wondering why I keep these as problems.
    b. Stage 4 usually brings consequences initially, then contradictions follow. For Walter we can see that only the *consequences* of recognising Stage 3 are

exposed. He is questioning himself as to why he is keeping these as problems. Recall from 'The Wobble', that the facilitator should wait for the doubt. The same applies here. If facilitating, allow the client time to discover the contradictions.

5. *Unravel* - the disentanglement or collapse of 'C', following up with the synthesis of 'B' and '!B'

    a. I do not know what connects them - but I am sure there is a root cause. Something at the bottom that ties them together
    b. Something *'connects'* all these elements, and for this to be true Walter is *'sure there is a root cause'*. If we consider that this statement is the moment that the boundary of C *unravels*, then Walter is now able to re-associate all this information.

6. *Emergence* - the new set of structures to allow Stage 5 to exist

    a. Work seems to be fraught with disharmony. I dislike the politics. I would like for us to focus on the goal. Disharmony is at the root - when I feel out of sync, then I eat, stress about money and work
    b. Notice that we now have new information and a new viewpoint on the original issue - where has *'fraught with disharmony'* suddenly come from? Walter can also see that this is now to do with *'politics'*, as well as discovering what it is he

would like. He then moves on to recognise that the *'unknown'* and *'don't know'* from Stages 3 and 4 is *'Disharmony is at the root'*. He finishes off with how all of this fits together and completes by reiterating his original construct of the system.

7. *Rest & Consolidation* - integration of this change
   a. Disharmony means that things are not working smoothly. It means that there is a risk of an emotional blow up. I want to avoid people blowing up - as I feel obligated to make it better for them. I need to make it OK
   b. Walter now expresses the meaning of what has just occurred. This is a higher level appreciation of his experience. We are also introduced to another level of Walter's situation which was not available previously, what else he wants and the structure of this. He wants *'to avoid people blowing up'*. There is also recognition of a not previously expressed structure of rules *'I feel obligated to make it better for them'*, *'I need to make it OK'*.

That concludes a full round of 7 stages.

We now begin again. Note that with this next series of questions the client looks at the reverse flow from issue to client,

"And what (else) does that know about you?"

Though, the first question Walter starts with on the second round is:

"And what do you know now?"

This offers him a new and fresh look at his issue:

1. *Recognition*
    a. That it is tied to disharmony and my need to make things OK for other people.
    b. Here we have a neat summary of what Walter stated in his last round.
2. *Effect*
    a. That I am scared of disharmony. Probably terrified of it.
    b. Walter is clearly making a statement of the effect this has on him.
3. *System & Form*
    a. His fear is being attacked and hurt. He wants to control the situation so that there is minimal risk. He wants to make sure people are OK.
    b. Notice that Walter has flipped his viewpoint here and is now referring to himself as a separate identity, the question structure can elicit this. Analysis of Walter's response again shows that this stage has the client looking at the context and the structures that hold the issue in place. For

Walter this is noticing that it is his *'fear'* which *'is being attacked and hurt'* and the requirement for *'control'*. His requirement *'to make sure people are OK'* is reiterated.

4. *Consequence & Contradiction*

    a. That he spends a lot of energy trying to prevent "bad" things from happening, instead of working to create good or better.
    b. Walter begins his answer with a consequence - *'he spends a lot of energy trying to prevent bad things'* - after which Walter presents the contradiction: *'working to create good or better.'* Here is a new part to the system. We can consider that this has appeared at the boundary of C, entering in from D - the Potential Space. Notice that the inverse of *'prevent bad'* is *'create good'*.

5. *Unravel*

    a. That he is totally controlled by others - what do they think about his weight? What they expect from him. He has totally vacated the ownership position, and is trying to figure out what others need.
    b. Walter continues to bring in contradictions - previously in Stage 3 it was him that was wanting control, now we see that it is others that control him. This is about *'what they expect from him'* and that he has vacated the *'ownership position'*.

This position has not been mentioned previously; is this vacation recognition of the unravelling? The questioning and confusions here are common in the 5th stage.

6. *Emergence*

   a. Controlling the uncontrollable is a losing proposition. People cannot be controlled. They will do things that may or may not be supportive. In the end, the focus is not where it needs to be.
   b. The statements made here are the restructuring of 'C'. These are firm concepts - *'Controlling the uncontrollable is a losing proposition', 'People cannot be controlled'*. Although these ideas may appear to have a negative slant, Walter's ideas about what is happening here have shifted; this is no longer about control, it's about focus. He finishes off with what needs to be addressed next.

7. *Rest & Consolidation*

   a. That his focus is on what other people want instead of what he wants. Instead of finding what he wants, he tries to justify everything, saying he could create it where he is. He is afraid of change.
   b. And now, Walter provides the consolidation and deeper meaning to the information that came out of Stage 6. Yet again, he finishes off with some new information: *'He is afraid of change'*.

From this short transcript we can see that each question stimulated our client into the next stage of awareness, but do not think that it is simply just the iteration of a question that does this (although this does offer benefit).

The facilitator's ability to spot where the client is, and time the delivery of the next question, is also very important to the success of Emergent Knowledge processing. Note that in the above transcript, facilitator input was not possible as it was run without facilitation via an online platform.

It's all about the Sequence

> *"All movements are accomplished in six stages, and the seventh brings return"*
>
> Syd Barrett (Pink Floyd) lyrics to Chapter 24

You may have noticed in Stage 7 of the second round in Walter's process that information was still emerging out of the consolidation stage; here we look at how this occurs.

The power to be utilised in the pattern is not in the numbers, but in the sequencing - it is this that drives the expansion of one's awareness to allow the mind to make sense of the problem or issue in another way.

This sequence is a neat description of the phases or stages of developing human awareness.

The purpose of the iteration is to move one's attention through these stages. The stages are not digital in nature, one doesn't instantly switch from one to another. Our attention responds more like a wave - for example, maybe it is currently in stage 4 with hints of 3 remaining and aspects of 5 rising. Sometimes the wave doesn't rise and fall at all, as the information gathered is not yet enough to stimulate a stage 5 deconstruction.

Continuing with this metaphor, observe the stages of a wave breaking and reaching the shoreline aligned with our six stages:

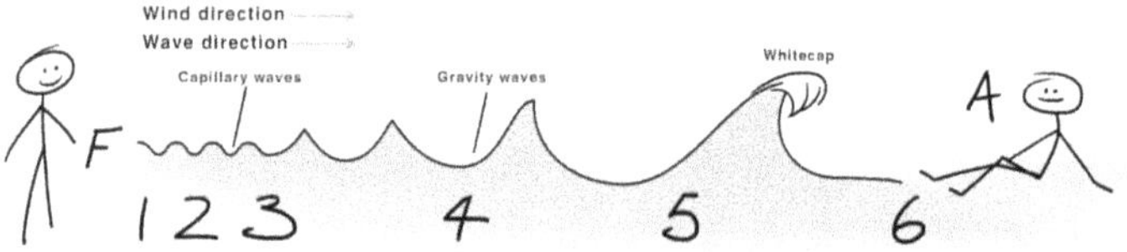

Stages of Wave Formation

We can imagine that the **Capillary Waves** (also known as ripples) are those initiated in the first three stages - thus these are the usual 'ripples of life', now consider that the client's attention is the **wave direction** and the iteration of the process provides the **wind**, it is necessary for both of these to be aligned in the same direction.

In stage 4 the client's system begins to shift and wobble, here **Gravity Waves** are generated; in oceanology these are waves that result when fluid is displaced from a position of equilibrium. This reflects what is happening for our client in the 'wobble' of stage 4. In stage 5, their system has culminated into a **Whitecap**, a breaking wave, and once this wave breaks (the Collapse/Unravelling), we move into stage 6, where the wave in its wake leaves behind on the shoreline some gift from the sea of the unconsciousness.

Summary of Revised Pattern

In summary, the revised naming of the stages are:

1. Recognition
2. Effect
3. System and Form
4. Consequence and Contradiction
5. Unravel
6. Emergence
7. Rest and Consolidation

The first letter of each stage provides us with a relative and useful acronym: RESCUER to help us remember each stage.

Another book will be published offering a deeper explanation into the above pattern and where it leads to after the 7th stage. I have now categorised another 14 stages, offering us:

21 Stages of Emergence

Another Client Transcript

Here follows a short transcript from another client.

Exercise

Read through this and note down the moments when you consider the client passes through each stage of their developing awareness.

1 - **Type into the box what you would like to work on**: repeated addictive behaviour patterns. I would like to stop doing them.

2 - **What do you know about that?** I have had compulsive types of behaviour for a long time, whether it has been food, tobacco, gaming, or checking the internet. I am aware that the behaviour keeps changing form. Whenever I change one behaviour, recently eating, I replace it with another (gaming) and have then swapped them again. The behaviour is healthier now than it has been, and yet at its core it remains the same break in concentration and activity to do something else.

3 - **And what else do you know about that?** I get a feeling in my chest which is quite sad and uncomfortable writing about it. I sometimes feel that I am in control and making choices myself and at other times experience it as something that I know is going to happen and may as well give up and let it happen. It is this which is often a trigger

for change. I am frustrated writing this because I got a response to the trigger for change sentence which was a little bit hopeless. Slight urge to cry appeared in my left eye

4 - **And what else do you know about that?** I get scared, don't want to end up like my mum, or my dad. I think too much, it may be that it helps me distract my head. Or not, I don't actually know. I am in the behaviour prison, keeping on building the walls and bars, not knowing what else to do.

5 - **And what else do you know about that?** I seem to refuse to believe that it could be as simple as stopping building the prison: could I really be so stupid that I have spent years doing something which was in reality pointless? I like solving puzzles and challenging my brain, and I am building a prison again! I want to both laugh and cry about how fucking ridiculous all of this is! I get a really good feeling about having found something to do instead and yet I know that it is just another iteration of the prison.

6 - **And what else do you know about that?** It feels like I am banging my head against a brick wall trying to find a solution, it hurts, and every now and again I change wall, or put something soft in the way, and then keep on banging. I keep saying that no one is stupid, but this behaviour is. Or is it just being human, and then I am negotiating again. I tell myself I should stop doing it, and currently find softer walls, but the headbanging continues.

7 - **And what else do you know about that?** The un-

comfortable feeling in my stomach increases with each question, as does the sadness, mostly around the eyes. It feels like the questions themselves are becoming a type of headbanging, reminding myself that I don't know the way to stop. The discomfort is why I want to stop, and that goes away quickly, so I start again...

8 - **And now what do you know?** I need help to find better questions and explore better solutions than headbanging.

9 - **And what is the difference between what you knew at the start and what you know now?** The feeling associated with headbanging is mostly in the stomach and guts, and it is a feeling of fear and inadequacy. I can't solve this one on my own, need to try something different. Or find something soft to hit my head on.

Patterning the Second Transcript

Here follows a brief outline structure to the above transcript relating to the Emergent pattern. Check this against your own notes.

1. Recognition - In the first statement the client simply states their recognition of the issue: *'repeated addictive behaviour patterns. I would like to stop doing them.'*
2. Effect - From the second statement, *'I change one behaviour, recently eating, I replace it with another'*, this can be seen as an explanation of the effect upon the client. As the client moves into the third statement, they are offering more effects upon themselves, with, *'I get a feeling in my chest..'* and *'I sometimes feel that I am in control...'*
3. System and Form - They then begin to bring form and structure to this, with, *'It is this which is often a trigger for change'*. They then finish off the third statement with more Effect, although this may also be part of the Consequences stage.
4. Consequences and Contradictions - The fourth statement provides us with, *'I get scared ...'*, *'I think too much ...'* These are the consequences of what has come so far. Then we get *'Or not'*, where the client now gets confused, *'I don't actually know'*, and then begins to offer the alternatives with references to a *'behaviour prison'* where they are *'building walls*

and bars, not knowing what else to do.' This idea is structurally different in that this is something the client is actually doing and not something that is being done only with their consent. This would fit in with being a contradiction.

5. Unravel - In the fifth statement we witness the unravelling, *'I seem to refuse to believe that it could be as simple as stopping building the prison'*. Both structures then begin to come together, *'Could I really be so stupid that I have spent years doing something which was in reality pointless?'*. Recall from the previous section that the client during the Unravelling step may become confused and question what has been happening. Of additional interest here is the dual contradiction of *"I want to both laugh and cry"*
6. Emergence - The client's idea of banging their head against the wall becomes apparent in their sixth statement, they are starting to restructure their model. With this comes thinking and questioning to test ideas and how things feel. This aspect of the process can be seen as the client works with what is happening to them in the moment. As they move into the seventh statement, they are bringing more attention onto *'headbanging'* and the structure of how this operates.
7. Rest - On the seventh statement the client is embodying the processing from stages #1 to #6 and acknowledges the structure of what is happening to them.

This transcript shows us how the stages of emergence can pass over into pre and post questions.

The patterning may also bring out the deeper symptoms. There is good evidence above to show that the headbanging and the associated feelings which have emerged in the client's system from the iterative questioning are within this category.

You can see that at question #8, which in a larger scale process would actually be utilised as a new #1 for the next set of questions, the client is providing the groundwork for the next stage in their journey.

Defining the Eternal Moment of Now

Here we are going to explore a new model to be added to the evolving Emergence canon. This model provides us with some tangible concepts and structures through which we may actually define, locate and experience the 'Eternal Moment of Now'.

It should be noted here that this model is a diversion from the classical Grovian Clean structures, even though it is based upon the work that David was working on at the end of his life.

In this way it echoes his work in Emergence; though I recognise that it is presented as a defined structure through which to view human behaviour, it therefore may be better placed in another category of models, than 'Clean'.

The application of the model is performed through the Emergent methodologies presented.

Four Fundamental Flows

History

Back in 2007 when I was modelling David's processes, he was exploring with clients how they were responding to their perceptions and understandings of their issue and their psychoactive landscape. This exploration can be observed in the 'Influences (Force Majeure)' section of Self-Alignment, where the client who has previously been working on exploring their Project (something that they want to work towards and achieve) now begins to explore how they interrelate to it.

It should be noted here that David was moving away from a pure Clean facilitation with his process, as his approach was utilising some generalised spatial metaphors based upon goal orientation.

Here David was utilising the basic motion constructs of *move away* and *move towards*:

1. *"And what (internal / external) influences move you away from this project?"*
2. *"And what (internal / external) influences move you towards this project?"*
3. *"And what (internal / external) influences stop you moving away from this project?"*
4. *"And what (internal / external) influences stop you moving towards this project?"*

The internal influences were explored first, then the external.

With respect to the above set of questions, we can visually represent this utilising the A to F model. As usual the client is at A and what they are working on is at B (in this instance their Project).

The Client and their Project

Internal

1. Something within A moves them away from B
2. Something within A moves them towards B
3. Something within A stops them moving away from B
4. Something within A stops them moving towards B

External

1. Something outside A moves them away from B
2. Something outside A moves them towards B
3. Something outside A stops them moving away from B

4. Something outside A stops them moving towards B

This dissection and exploration of influences has proven both useful and informative over the years, though through multiple usage of these questions I had always felt aspects were missing from the exploration, so over the last few years I've focused on the further development of this area.

Searching for the Missing Pieces

This began by looking for what was missing by asking what the purpose of the influence was in each case, and noticing that, when the client had something to be wanted / gained, this generally resulted in a move towards motion, or, when something was unwanted / to be refused, this resulted in a move away motion.

On a basic analysis of the internal influences the following structures emerged:

1. A does not want something from B
2. A wants something from B
3. A does not want something from B but cannot stop it
4. A wants something from B but cannot get it

The same is true for the external influences, though these are not controlled by the client (A).

As the constructs of #1 and #2 are resident in all four questions I wanted to define the core structures of these first. Considering the way the client is operating in both of these scenarios, these constructs were named as Oppose (#1) and Expose (#2) respectively, a full definition of each follows.

In Oppose

Oppose: Set against, resist, obstruct

from **OB**- meaning 'towards, against, in the way of' and **POSE** meaning 'to place'

- A is actively 'against' something coming towards them from B
  - B has something and A must not get it
  - To achieve this, A must **push** against something from B

Some Ideas are Forcefully Opposed

Examples from A:

"I don't want to know."

"Stop treating me this way!"

"Please, can you just leave me alone."

In Expose

Expose: Disclose, reveal, show

from **EX-** meaning 'out of' and **POSE** meaning 'to place'

- A is actively 'for/pro' something coming toward them from B
  - B has something and A must get it
  - To achieve this, A must **pull** on something from B

Exposing using Interrogation

Examples from A:

"Was it good? Tell me, come on what happened?"

"What else is there?"

"You better tell us what you did."

Expanding the Search

These ideas led to a greater understanding of the original questions (#3 and #4) which were designed to discover the internal and external conflicts a client was experiencing. Understanding the structure of these questions may get a little confusing; as in #3, where the client's Oppose (move away) motion is up against another internal Oppose (stop), and, in #4 the client's Expose (move towards) motion is working against another internal Oppose (stop).

Realising the potential confusion (as you will see later this is because both of these structures are of the same order), I stepped away from David's original questions and focused only on the basic motions and flows occurring to and from A and B themselves:

Over at position B we have the client's Project, which at the beginning of the Self-Alignment journey is described as something that is thrown forward (from Latin *pro-* meaning 'forth' and *jacere* meaning to 'throw'). However, once the Project is 'thrown out' there, from the client's perspective it (the project) is also projecting itself, i.e. it is flowing itself back to the client, for example this could be experienced as seeing the benefits and flaws in the project or the required steps needed to achieve it. Basically everything to do with the Project that the client is aware of and becoming aware of.

Therefore, there are particular aspects of this Project that the client perceives as flowing towards them at A. Following this logic, there must be aspects of the client that also flow out or impose themselves upon the Project. This was the beginning of locating the missing pieces.

The search was nearly complete as I had now recognised that both A and B were able to Oppose and Expose, and it now followed that both could project or 'Impose'. Here were three clear ways of interacting. This was making perfect sense, especially when transposing A and B to being two people in a relationship.

This idea of projection has been given the title 'Impose'.

In Impose

Impose: Lay or inflict, force (oneself) upon the attention of

from **IM-** meaning 'in, within, internal' and **POSE** meaning 'to place'

- A is actively 'for/pro' something going into B
  - A has something and B must get it
  - To achieve this, A must **push** something into B

An Idea Culturally Imposed

Examples from A:

"Let me tell you about ..."

"I hope you're listening to me, this is very important..."

On defining Impose the final piece was about to naturally and logically fall into place.

A New Insight

On having these three structural definitions, I then defined the logical opposite of Impose and all was revealed:

- A is actively 'against' something going into B
  - A has something and B must not get it
  - To achieve this, A must **pull** on something so B is unable to get it

Thus the fourth, 'uncannily' hidden piece was:

Concealing / Hiding / Restraining

Conceal: Keep secret, refrain from disclosing

from **CON-** meaning 'with, together, jointly and completely' and **CEAL** (*celare*) meaning 'to hide'

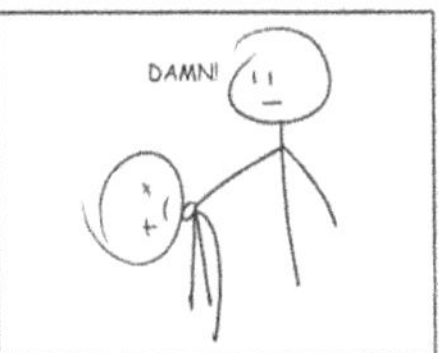

The Spy's Ultimate Concealment

Examples from A:

"There's nothing to tell really."

"I'm leaving"

"No comment"

Defining Two Mechanisms of Interaction

These four fundamental flows may be sorted into two sets of behaviour or mechanisms of interaction that either side (or node) of this basic 2-node system (A & B) could adopt:

- a destination side
- a source side

Both of these sides have the ability to produce a flowing-out and a flowing-in behaviour as previously described. A distinction is to be made here between A & B nodes and Source & Destination nodes as they are two distinct categories. An A node is capable of being both Source and Destination, likewise so can B.

At this point we are only focusing on a single interaction of one node being the Source and one being the Destination. To help in this explanation we will consider that there is an item (a jewel) held by the source node. Utilising a physical object like this provides a good base for developing from. We will now drop the usage of A and B for the moment.

The fundamental flows in and out for each node are shown graphically overleaf.

The Destination Flows

The destination *flows out* to the source, when **Opposing** the jewel from the source. This is akin to our original 'Move Away' construct, where more space between nodes is intended.

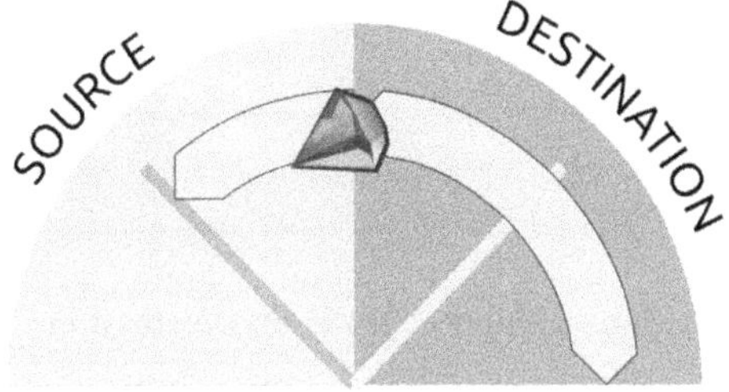

Destination Opposes Jewel at Source

The destination *flows in* from the source to itself when **Exposing** the jewel from the source. This is related to our original 'Move Towards' construct, where less space between nodes is intended.

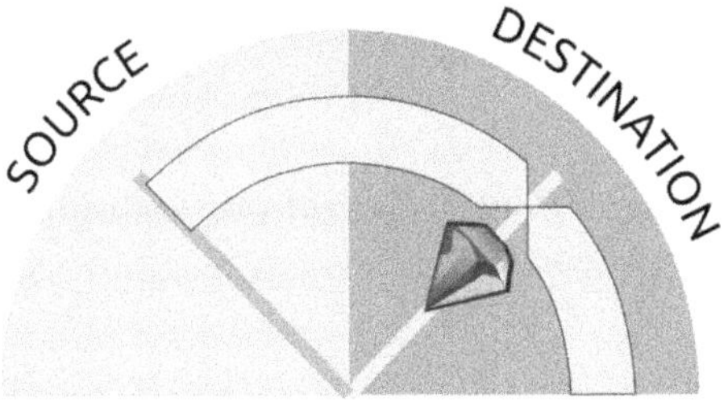

Destination Exposes Jewel from Source

The Source Flows

The source *flows out* to the destination, when **Imposing** the jewel on the destination.

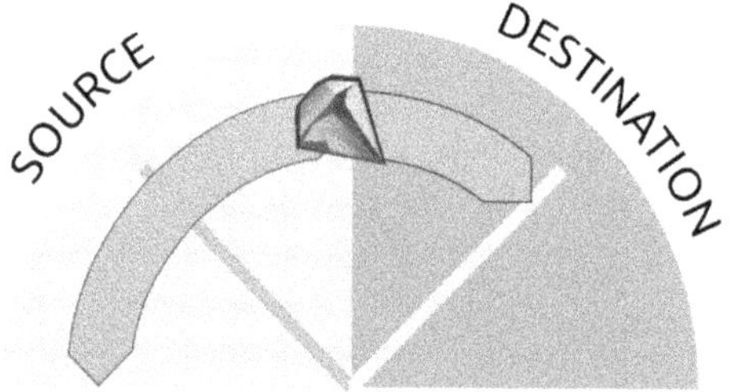

Source Imposes Jewel on Destination

The source *flows in* to itself, when **Concealing** the jewel from the destination.

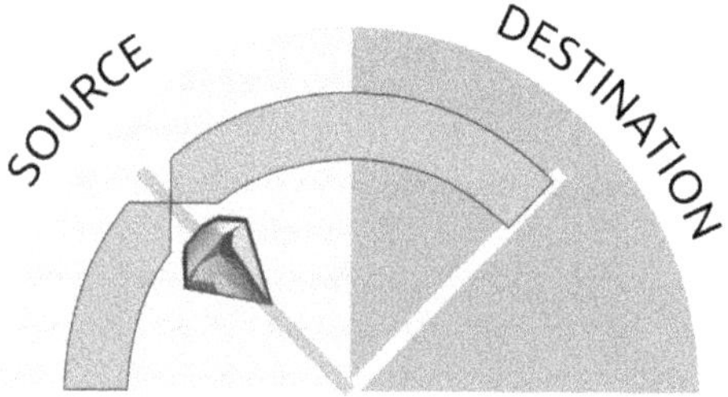

Source Conceals Jewel from Destination

The Destination Set

The node associated with this set is referenced as the Destination or Receiver node in the system.

Be aware that although we have used the terms Oppose and Expose to provide an overarching description for the behavioural flows or expressions of this node, these simple terms do not and can not fully express the full range of available actions and reactions which are available or possible to the individual.

Instead, we must look upon this range as a long spectrum to better understand the available expressions. To do this we must first accept that the terms 'Oppose' and 'Expose' are diametrically (polar) opposite to each other, with the absolute expression of Oppose at one end and the absolute expression of Expose at the other with a full gradient of expressions in between.

This spectrum can be seen on the chart below as the horizontal axis, the Oppose side of the axis is Flowing-Out, this is represented with an arrow pointing away from the axis. The Expose side of the axis is Flowing-In represented with an arrow pointing towards the axis. At the central 0%, there is no flow, a point of stillness with no action or reaction, the 100% marks are the maximum flows possible. The angled areas behind are an abstract representation of all the possible expressions available to the Destination.

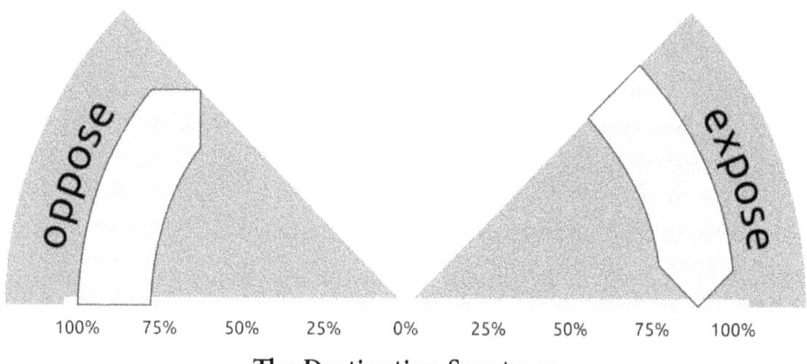

The Destination Spectrum

Below are some examples for each of the expressions. The numerical figures chosen are approximations of where they may sit on the spectrum, as everyone will have their own interpretation of where these exist.

Oppose is a determined flow outwards initiated by the destination node

- The intention is to stop something (i.e. an idea) coming in from source (owner of that idea)
    - 25% : Disinterest in the idea
    - 50% : Dismissal, dejection, openly averse towards the idea
    - 75% : Hostility towards the owner in order to stop the idea
    - 100% : Anger, physical violence, even destruction of the owner to stop the idea (e.g. a war against terrorism)

Expose is a determined flow inwards initiated by the destination node

- The intention is to start something (i.e. information) coming out from source (owner of that information)
  - 25% : Interested to know the information
  - 50% : Requesting, negotiating to get the information
  - 75% : Demanding to have the information from the owner
  - 100% : Taking the information by force (e.g. interrogation)

The Source Set

The node associated with this set is considered to be the Source or Provider node of the system. The expression of this node exists somewhere on the Impose-Conceal spectrum, shown as the angled areas on the chart below, which is designed the same as the Destination Spectrum shown previously.

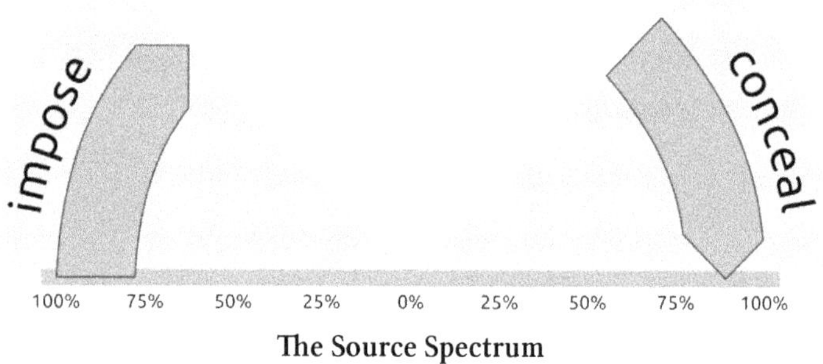

The Source Spectrum

Examples of these flows are given below, again the values given are approximate.

Impose is a determined flow outwards by the source node

- The intention is to get something (i.e. an idea) going into the destination
  - 25% : Presenting information
  - 50% : Talking over another and giving the idea irrespectively
  - 75% : Coercing or intimidating another to accept the idea

  - 100% : Forcing another to accept the idea (e.g. threats, violence, torture)

Conceal is a determined flow inwards by the source node

- The intention is to stop something (i.e. a secret) going out to the destination
  - 25% : Not mentioning it, creating a distraction
  - 50% : Turning away, ignoring
  - 75% : Shutting down, secreting, withholding, suppressing, hiding
  - 100% : Destroying or vanishing self to stop the revelation (e.g. suicide)

We can see from the above four flows that expressions occurring at the extreme ends (100%) of the spectrums result in serious unwanted scenarios, unfortunately in life these do occur.

These actions are a last chance or final attempt at fulfilling one's intentions. We may consider that as one moves from the centre point where there is choice and opportunity, the further out we go the less choice and opportunity there appears to be. Thus, the potential final choice at the extreme.

The Spectrums and Volition

> *"Between stimulus and response there is a space. In that space is our power to choose our response. In our response lies our growth and our freedom."*
>
> Stephen R. Covey

As one moves from a still point on the spectrum towards a particular expression, we can observe the direction and level of an individual's volition is directly related to the level of importance or necessity required.

What we are looking at then is a 'Scale of Volition' and this is finely graduated, the differences between each referenced zone on the scale may be subtle, however if one looks at either end of the scales there are significant differences of how we execute our behaviour.

A Scale of Volition

To help in understanding this let us breakdown the full range of volition that is being presented into four separate levels or zones. Moving up and out from the zero point on our spectrum we enter the first zone: **Care-free or Natural**, where we perform and act with no hindrance, simply doing what is required to achieve our goal. This zone also comprises the elements of fun and playfulness.

Let us now imagine that some hindrance to achieving our goal has been located, at this moment we have entered the second zone: **Attentive and Focused**, where a little more effort is going to be required and we must start to apply ourselves and our attention to achieve our goal. There is still an element of fun in the engagement, though now we can expect to see purpose and planning involved.

As we persist in our quest here, we discover that what we actually want is further out of reach and in some ways is perhaps being withheld from us, we have entered the third zone: **Determination**. Now we must up our game and begin really making an effort to get to where we want to be, the actions we take here will become more intense and more determined. Now, we are becoming serious about the issue at hand, any playfulness left over from the prior zones is now going away or perhaps it has gone altogether.

If the affront to us achieving what we want continues there is the possibility that we enter the fourth zone: **Necessitate**, where force and 'called for' actions are administered. Here we are literally causing what we want to have happen with perhaps little or no regard to others and the consequences following on. 'What has to be done has to be done' and 'The ends justify the means' are expressions of this zone. The requirements to get into the zone are both positive and negative, for instance 'The Civil Rights Movement'.

The Four Zones

1. Natural and Care-Free
2. Attentive and Focused
3. Determined
4. Necessitate

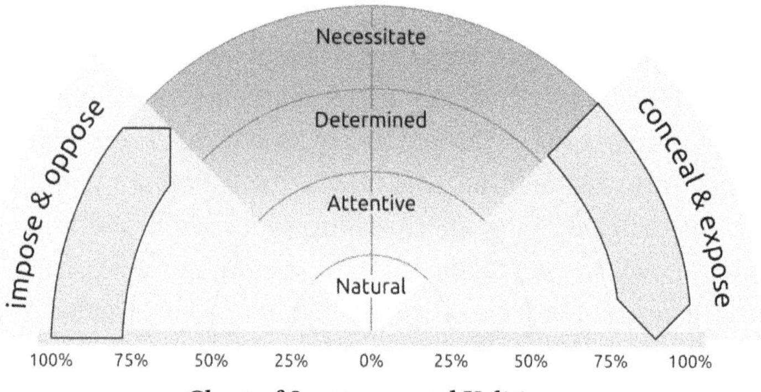

Chart of Spectrums and Volition

At any point whilst moving through these zones we are able to pause and make a choice as to whether we wish to persist or cease our interaction. This is the space that Stephen Covey is talking about in his quote above. Though it would seem that the further out we get the harder this is to achieve as our choices are becoming limited and our volition to achieve is increasing. Pausing and taking stock, taking the time to look for more options and other solutions really helps.

Here follows some example expressions of the Four Flows alongside this Scale of Volition. We will refer back to these in the next section.

Tables of Example Expressions

Source Expressions

Zones	Impose	Conceal
Natural	Invitation	Distraction and Diversion
Attentive	Request and Influence	Disguise and Deception
Determined	Urge and Coerce	Withhold and Retain
Necessitate	Projection, Insistence and Demands	Restriction, Secreting and Coverup

Destination Expressions

Zones	Expose	Oppose
Natural	Interest	Disinterest
Attentive	Inquisitive and Curiosity	Indifference and Incurious
Determined	Discern and Ascertain	Disinclination and Objection
Necessitate	Exposing, Revelation and Force	Rejection and Force

Modal Operators in the Zones

- Natural and Care-Free
  - Modal Operators of Possibility or Impossibility
    - able to / unable to
    - can / can not
- Attentive and Focused
  - Modal Operators of Probability / Improbability
    - might / might not
    - could / could not
- Determination
  - Modal Operators of Desirability / Undesirability
    - like to / not like to
    - wish to / not wish to
    - want to / not want to
    - will / will not
- Necessitate
  - Modal Operators of Necessity
    - supposed to / not supposed to
    - should / should not
    - have to / not have to
    - must / must not

Bringing the Sets Together

Now that we have explored each of these flows (Oppose, Expose, Conceal and Impose) as independent elements, it is time to bring them together to see how they interrelate with each other.

To do this we shall allocate each source set to each destination set, creating four unique interplays:

- Impose & Expose
- Impose & Oppose
- Conceal & Expose
- Conceal & Oppose

On doing this we will see that the resulting interaction of the flows within each of the four interplays creates two distinct categories:

1. Complementary Interplays
2. Conflicting Interplays

I propose that these four interplays and the structure of these new categories are fundamental in understanding relationships; in fact, in understanding any interconnectedness of two or more entities.

Let us now explore these in more detail.

Complementary Interplays

These are where the interplay of flows is 'Agreeable' to both sides and the result is 'Mutually Beneficial', we can see that in both cases an outflow is accompanied by an inflow, its matching counterpart, thus the flows between source and destination are open and unhindered.

In both cases, there is a positive response from both parties:

Impose & Expose

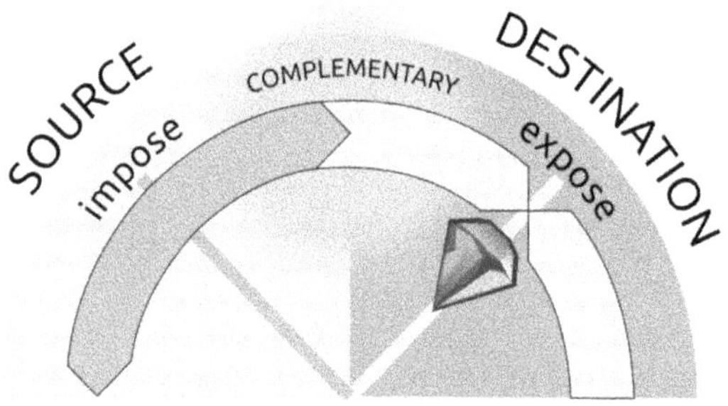

(S) Impose *(out)* >> > >> *(in)* Expose (D)

Source is giving the jewel to Destination

Destination is wanting the jewel from Source

- Source willingly gives and Destination willingly receives
  - like having birthday money given to you from your Gran

- like a good conversation or consensual sex (flowing back and forth usually works best!)
- like successfully learning or teaching something

Conceal & Oppose

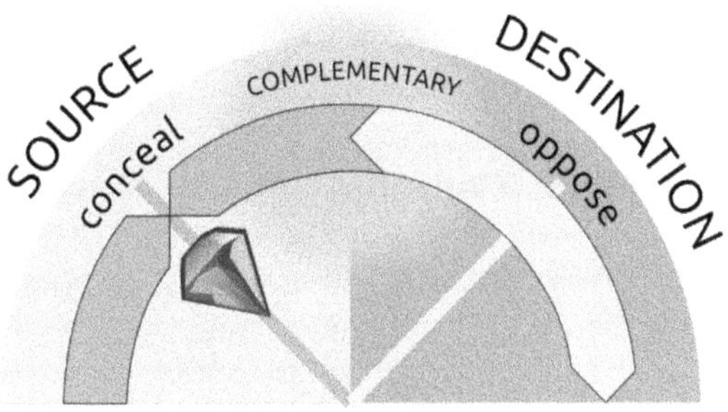

(S) Conceal *(in)* << < << *(out)* Oppose (D)

Source is holding the jewel back from Destination

Destination is averse to the jewel from Source

- Source doesn't give and Destination doesn't want to receive
  - like supporting someone on a diet
  - like living in denial of your partner's secret 'extra-curricular' activities
  - like a mutual breakup of a relationship

Conflicting Interplays

This is where the interplay is a 'Struggle for Power' and the result is an eventual 'Overpowering' or submission from one or both parties. We can see that each flow is accompanied by its matching flow in both cases, therefore creating hindered and stifled flow patterns.

In both, there is a negative response from both parties; neither is getting what they intend.

Impose & Oppose (Collision)

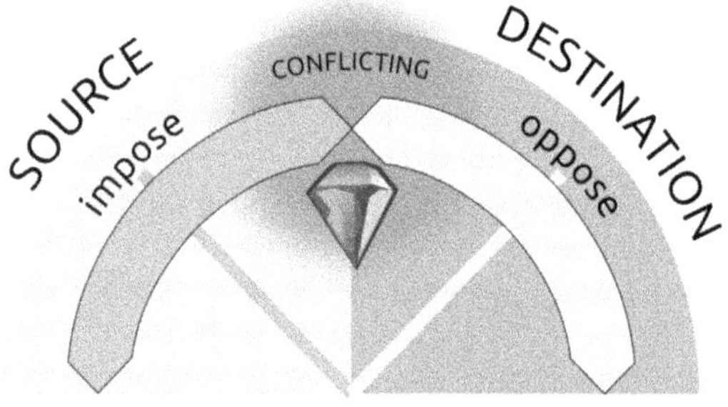

(S) Impose *(out)* >> | << *(out)* Oppose (D)

Source is giving the jewel to Destination

Destination is averse to the jewel from Source

- Source gives and Destination doesn't want to receive
  - like a game of 'hot-potato'
  - like physical abuse
  - like refusing help from a friend

Conceal & Expose (Divergence)

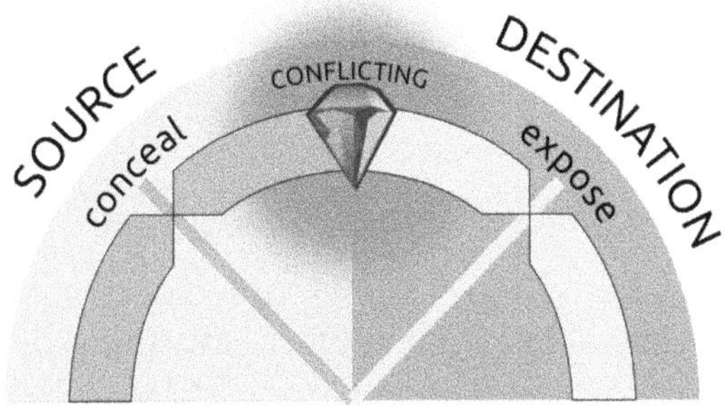

(S) Conceal *(in)* << * >> *(in)* Expose (D)

Source is holding the jewel back from Destination

Destination is wanting the jewel from Source

- Source doesn't give and Destination wants to receive
  - like a game of hide-and-seek or cops and robbers
  - like cross-examining the accused in a court of law
  - like a child not sharing their toys

It is within these conflicting scenarios that most defining moments are generally created. When one side completely overpowers the other to such a degree that they are forced to drop their position, and in doing so, they succumb to the dominating side, this can result in trauma.

Examples of Overpowering and Submission

Overpowering in Conflicting Flows

- Impose: Forcing something on another they do not want
- Conceal: Withholding something from another they want
- Expose: Taking from another something they do not want to give
- Oppose: Refusing to accept something another wants to force on them

Submission in Conflicting Flows

- Imposed: Having something forced upon them by another they did not want
- Concealed: Having something withheld by another they want
- Exposed: Having something taken by another they did not want to give
- Opposed: Having something refused by another they wanted to force on them

The Interplay of Expressions

To deepen our understanding of these interplays, let us remind ourselves of the Tables of Example Expressions from earlier (go back and quickly check this) to explore a hypothetical scenario, starting off in a Complementary interplay and look at how that may shift and sway towards a Conflicting interplay and back again or, if unhandled may escalate out of control.

The School Classroom

To begin we have our teacher (The Source) inviting information (Imposing) to the interested (Exposing) student (The Destination), all is well and everyone is in the 'Natural Zone'. Whilst this is happening and working well then neither side needs to shift or is required to move into the 'Attentive Zone'.

Though let us say that now the student misses some understanding of what is being presented, they are no longer receiving information from the teacher - therefore their perception is that the Source is no longer providing (Conceal). This is now a low-level Conflicting interplay. To reinitiate and get this flow moving again the student moves into the 'Attentive Zone' and becomes more inquisitive and curious, most likely resulting in asking a pertinent question.

When the teacher responds appropriately and is attending to the student's needs, they increase their intention into the

'Attentive Zone' and resolve the misunderstanding. Thus bringing the system back to a Complementary interplay and once the student receives the required information. Both teacher and student can drop back to the 'Natural Zone' to continue.

Now, if the student had asked the question, but was still not getting the required understanding, here the teacher remains in Conceal and is now holding back the required information which the student really wants, to understand the subject. The teacher now appears to be failing them.

The student may now be motivated to move into the 'Determination Zone' and begin to interrupt the teacher making the required actions to ascertain the required information. If this is resolved, great! If not the student again moves, this time into the zone of 'Necessitate', as their teacher is proving unable to provide as required. It appears that the teacher is actually restricting the flow of required information. The student may now end up reporting the teacher to a higher authority in order to achieve their goal of learning.

On the flip side, let us follow the same process of shifting from the teacher's perspective.

From what was a good flowing lecture the teacher recognises that their students are losing interest and are becoming noisy (Oppose), they move into the 'Attentive Zone' and request the attention or change their approach to influence the students into engaging again.

The teacher and students are now in a Conflicting interplay, the students with no interest in the teacher or subject move into the 'Attentive Zone' of Oppose, they start to simply ignore the teacher and do their own thing. As the teacher's requests have fallen on 'deaf ears' the teacher follows suit and moves into the 'Determination Zone' to attempt to coerce the students back.

It is here that the teacher may lose the class entirely with the students becoming unruly as they push back due to moving into the 'Determination Zone' where they now begin to object to the teacher. The following 'Necessitate Zone' brings shouting, demands and people leaving by force or of their own volition, tables may be turned and things said or done that could be regretted later.

A Proposition

Let me propose that when a conflicting interplay of this level (Necessitate) has begun, if we are able to recognise where the other party is in relation to ourselves. We may purposefully adopt their complementary position to defuse a potential disasterous scenario. Then once we have both dropped back to the 'Natural Zone' and the tensions and heightened emotions have reduced, we may be able to discuss and start to make positive moves towards the original purpose. This next section looks at this in greater detail and provides a working model of how this mechanism works.

Determinism - Self and Other

Each of the expressions we have looked at are representations of our self-determinism, whether we are the source point or the destination point. It should be recognised that when we hold a particular self-determined position in an interaction, we are also holding the complementary other-determined position out there for the opposite party to be or become.

In a conflicting scenario, this is a requirement to have our opponent change their self-determined position to our other-determined one, or for us to change our self-determined position to the other-determined idea of our opponent, this demand or at least requirement to change creates the conditions for conflict.

For example, a source point (A) is currently in the Impose position in conflict with a destination point (B) in the Oppose position. The other-determined expressions of these two points are:

- A working towards the complementary needs to have B adopt the Expose position
- B working towards it's complementary needs to have A adopt the Conceal position

Both of these changes are a 180 degree reversal of the individual's current position on the spectrum, hence why matters sometimes rapidly escalate into heavily charged situations and the eventual succumbing of one of the sides.

A real world example of this is the development of the Cold War between the USA and USSR, where one side would make a move to establish their power and through this expected the other side to step back. For instance in 1949 the USA began imposing themselves in the Eastern Bloc, and implemented a propoganda radio station designed to peacefully bring a demise to the communist system there, to achieve this the Eastern Bloc and the USSR would have to move into an accepting Expose position, the counter-position of Oppose.

The USSR remaining in opposition, pushed back against this and other alliances with an increase and threat of nuclear power intending that the USA pull out and stop their imposition, an expression of the Conceal position. However, the USA didn't and followed suit increasing their nuclear arsenal, this was a further increase of the USA's volition within the Impose position.

This to and froing continued for many, many years, creating more wars and an ever increasing threat to humanity. In 1990 we saw the eventual dissolution of the USSR and the Communist Party surrendering its monopoly of state power. The Cold War was over.

The Three-Node Problem

You may recall from the beginning of this section that in the original influence questions (#3 and #4) from Self-Alignment, the structures of Oppose and Expose were presented together.

From the Four Flows model we can see that with a simple 2-node system this is a difficult scenario to build, for both A and B would have to be Destination Nodes. In this regard we have moved from a two-node problem to a three-node problem.

We have the original two nodes A and B, and now a new node which we shall call 'G' (so that we do not give two references to C in the A to F Model).

G has the potential to influence and 'Guide' the flows between A and B. The original two questions (#3 and #4) from the Force Majeure section in Self-Alignment can now be re-created using this new model as follows:

3. *"And what external influences stop you moving away from this project?"*

This now becomes:

- What must you make sure you do not get from that?
- And, who or what is opposing that?

4. *"And what external influences stop you moving towards this project?"*

This now becomes:

- What must you make sure you get from that?
- And, who or what is opposing that?

Other questions which look to discover G in the network are:

- And, what is in between you and that?
- And, what is around you / that?

Utilising the structure of a Three-Node system the original question set may be further expanded to explore all of A's four flows to and from B, along with G's four flows towards each one of these flows. And, if we so wished B's four flows could also be explored in the same manner. Although so far from experience, the application of this method applied to A is all that has been required for a resolution to the clients issue to emerge.

This process is advanced and quite indepth requiring training to deliver, thus it is only available on Emergent Knowledge training courses and through personal sessions with a trained facilitator. The basic structure of the Four Flows model is presented in Process #3.

The Chart of Interactions

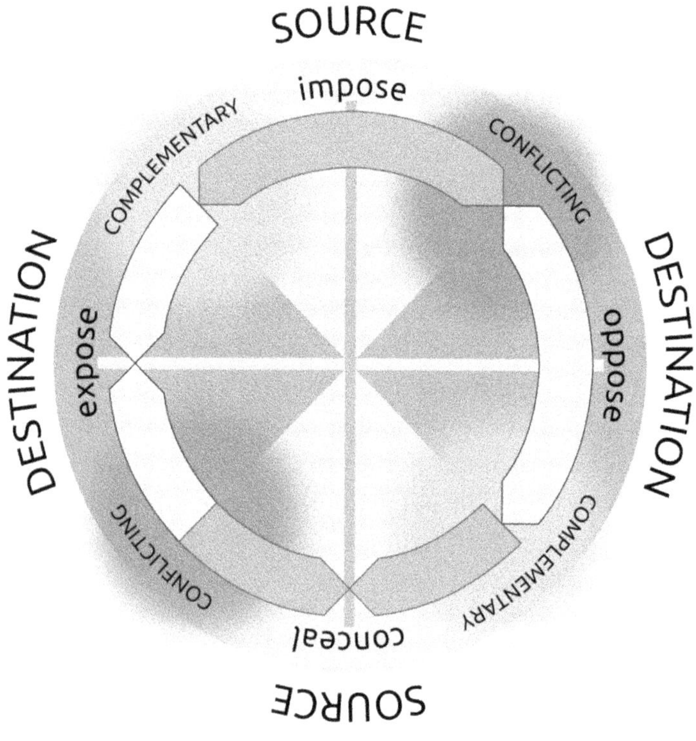

Chart of Interactions

Above, we have the 'Chart of Interactions'. This chart provides a full representation of all the flows and interactions possible, in all the zones of volition.

The horizontal axis represents the Destination Spectrum, running from Expose on the left to Oppose on the right.

Vertically, through the zero point, we run the vertical axis representing the Source Spectrum running from Impose at the top to Conceal at the bottom.

On each side of these axes are shown with arrows the direction of flow the relevant expression exhibits. Thus, the Oppose side flows outwards above and below the axis towards both sides of the source axis. We can see that the Oppose (out)flow below the axis is complementary as it connects with the source (in)flow of Concealing, and that above is conflicting as it connects with the source (out)flow of Impose.

The chart provides a clear visual representation of how all these flows work and interact.

Spend some time looking over this chart and developing a deep understanding of what it represents, then watch a movie or your favourite TV series, and notice where the characters are on the chart. Notice how their position determines the resulting reactions in the film. Are you able to recognise what the focus of their intention is on? What is it they are working to achieve? How far will they go to achieve it?

See the final section in this chapter on Little Red Riding Hood to read a breakdown of this classic children's story.

Expressions at the extremes of the axes are damaging, and become less so as they tend towards the centre, where there is little to no flow.

This brings us all full circle.

The Eternal Moment of Now

Up until this point, the client has only been allocated to the Source position or the Destination position. Let us now recognise that as humans we are capable of being both in the same moment. We are *transceivers*, meaning we are transmitters and receivers of information. This happens constantly on many levels. Let us then apply this idea to the Chart of Interactions and this notion of Inner Peace.

When we allocate both axes of the chart to an individual, we can see that it is here in this centre point where the expression of Inner Peace sits.

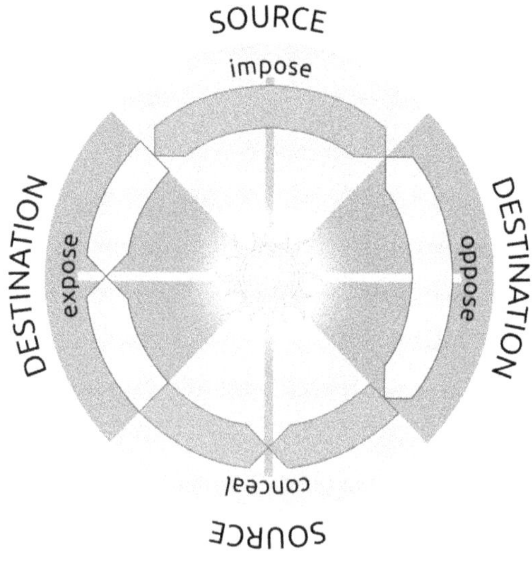

The Centre Point of Inner Peace

For the individual who effortlessly resides at this point there is no requirement to prove or present themselves in any way (impose), they have no requirement to hide anything or turn away from anything (conceal). They're aware that they have no requirement to stop anything happening (oppose) and no requirement to have anything happen or come to them (expose). All of these expressions when made are made with known intention.

Thus, a state of no ego, no judgement, no resistance, no avoidance - just pure beingness. Here is also a reference to Wu Wei in Lao Tzu's Tao, for here is 'actionless action' or 'effortless action'; being in the flow of the Universe, where we are swimming with rather than against the currents.

The Seven Attitudes of Mindfulness

The above centre point on the chart relates to and provides a model to understanding the classic 'Seven Attitudes of Mindfulness'.

- Non-Judgement
- Non-Striving
- Acceptance
- Beginner's Mind
- Letting Go
- Patience
- Trust

Let us now take each of these attitudes and reflect on their relationship to this new model.

Non-Judgement

Judgement is representative of the **Impose** flow. Here an idea generated within the individual flows out to make thoughts and considerations about something out there. Non-Judgement is when an Impose flow no longer occurs.

Non-Striving

Striving is representative of **Expose**, where the individual is focused on having something come to them or to happen. Non-Striving is the recognition of this aspect being clear and free of intention.

Acceptance

We can have acceptance of many things as well as ourselves and others. In Acceptance we are no longer **Opposing** what is within and outside of us.

Beginner's Mind

Coming at life from the stand point of the Beginner's Mind, shows us that we hold no preconceptions - we are free of our past. It is as though we are witnessing life for the first time. In this manner, we have some aspects of all four of the flows. We may, for the convenience of allocation, direct the idea of the Beginner's Mind to the absence of the **Conceal** flow, where one no longer hides from their past or has to 'stay out of the limelight'. One can comfortably just be, as though being for the first time.

Although accepting the above is ok, there is more than sufficient information here to propose an 8th Attitude which encompasses the **Conceal** flow specifically, perhaps 'Non-Constraint'.

Letting Go

The thought of simply Letting Go relates to achieving release on all the above four flows. Allowing oneself to converge on the centre point, from the sense of being the source and also being the receptor, letting go of all need and intention to flow in or out in either form.

Patience

The acceptance of knowing that moving from the upper zones on the spectrums to the centre point may take time, and it may require the energy and effort of overcoming and releasing the presenting issues that hinder this journey. Patience is a virtue, they say, for giving ourselves and others the time to bring about the changes in their lives to move from acting in Necessity, Requirement, Desire, then Naturally and finally to the zero centre point of peace.

Trust

Encompassing all of this is the trust in self, and the nature of our expressions, that we are able to experience this Eternal Moment.

Little Red Riding Hood

To offer some examples of how the Four Flows model fits in with a vast variety of experiences, here is presented a short breakdown of the story of Little Red Riding Hood by Charles Perrault from The Tales of Mother Goose, annotated with the Four Flows model, be warned this is based on the original unsanitised version, there is no happy ending.

The story revolves around a girl called Little Red Riding Hood. Red walks through the woods to deliver food (custard and butter) to her sickly Grandmother.

- Here we have Red as the Source flowing out, on an Impose out-flow, with food towards her Grandma as the Destination who needs the food, which is an Expose in-flow. This is a Complementary interaction.

A bad wolf wants to eat the girl and the food in the basket.

- The wolf is introduced as another Destination for the Source (Red and food), although with much greater intentions of eating. The wolf coming into the story also shows us the potential complexities of having a three-node system.

He secretly stalks her behind the trees and bushes and doesn't immediately eat her as there are others in the woods.

- To hide himself and not be killed, the wolf Conceals (Source) himself. Anyone else in the woods is Opposed to wolves, so by not witnessing him we again have a Complementary interaction.

He slyly approaches Little Red Riding Hood and asks where she is going, Red naively tells him.

- The wolf first reveals himself and attempts to Expose information from Red, then after he Exposes the information from Red with his convincing manner and as she succumbs to his subtle deception, she then reveals, by Imposing, her true intentions to the wolf. Another Complementary interaction even if performed with bad intentions.

The wolf then suggests that he and Red race to her Grandmother's house to see who can get there first, which she agrees to.

- The wolf Imposes his deception upon her, his deceptive Impose fits perfectly with Red's previously Exposed information and her childish nature, so she follows along with it, her acceptance is an Expose inflow resulting in another Complementary interaction.

He goes directly to the Grandma's house and gains entry by pretending to be the girl and promptly swallows Grandma whole and waits for the girl, disguised as Grandma.

- The wolf again uses Concealing to deceive the Grandma and then fully (Volition 100%) Imposes himself upon her by attacking her. He finally becomes the Destination of Grandma by devouring her completely (a full 100% Expose). Concealing himself again afterwards, dressing up as Grandma to trick Red. This full Impose on Grandma is the first Conflicting interaction we see, though no Oppose is mentioned.

When Red arrives, she notices that her Grandma looks very strange. Little Red says "What great arms you have got!" ("All the better to hug you with", responds the wolf), "Goodness, what great legs you have got!" ("That is to run the better", responds the wolf), "And what great ears you have got!" ("All the better to hear you with", responds the wolf), and lastly, "What great teeth you have got!" ("All the better to eat you up!", responds the wolf), at which point the wolf jumps out of the bed and eats her all up too.

- When Red notices that Grandma looks strange, she begins to Expose the wolf, the wolf continuing to Conceal his true identity through all the questions is waiting for the right moment to attack and turn the tables, his deceitful Imposed answers are given to lull poor Red into a false sense of security by creating a Complementary interaction. Then, the wolf suddenly becomes the Source and Imposes himself upon Red by attacking her, and just like Grandma, the wolf becomes the final Destination for poor Red - the final Conflict.

THE END

As already stated, in this version of the story there is no direct Oppose out-flow mentioned. For us to include this flow we would have to assume there is an unmentioned Oppose flow in the devouring of the Grandma and Red.

It is interesting however, that in later versions of the story a Woodcutter was introduced whom fulfilled this role and killed the wolf and retrieved Red and her Grandma from inside it.

PRACTICAL II

- Process #3 - 'The Basic Four Flows'
- Process #4 - 'The Eternal Moment of Now'

Process #3 - The Basic Four Flows

Here follows an introductory process designed to open up and begin an exploration of the Four Fundamental Flows with respect to an existing condition.

This process provides the base structure to deeper and more involved processes in this category.

Introduction

This is a simple process to run for the beginning facilitator. Once the client has detailed what it is they would like to work on, the iterative question sets look to explore what is happening in each of the four flows, from the client's (A) perspective.

Clean Space methodology is utilised throughout, thus all answers are generally spoken first then represented on paper and placed in space.

After each iterative question set, a new Recognition Stage is initiated to keep the client in the present moment. Each time the new statement is given a location and the client moves to where they are in relationship to it.

Allow the client to freely move around the space as they feel necessary.

The Basic Four Flows Process

- *"Represent what you'd like to work on, place this where it belongs"*
- *"And where are you now in relationship to that?"*
- *"And what could this space be called?"*

Four Flows from A's Viewpoint

Standing in your space run through the following question sets. Answering, writing down and placing this answer for each question:

Check the Four Flows

1. *"And what must you not get from that?"*
    - "Place that where it belongs"*
2. *"And what must you get from that?"*
    - "Place that where it belongs"*
3. *"And what must you make sure that doesn't get from you?"*
    - "Place that where it belongs"*
4. *"And what must you make sure that does get from you?"*
    - "Place that where it belongs"*

New Recognition Stage

Download, Upload and create a new Viewpoint

a. *"And what do you know now about all of this?"*
b. *"Place that where it belongs"*
c. *"And place yourself where you are now in relationship to that?"*
d. *"And what could this space be called?"*

Iterate

Repeat the Four Flows and Recognition stages five more times

Finishing Off

1. *"Choose a new space outside of all of this"*
2. *"And what do you know from here?"*
3. *"And what else do you know from here?"* x 5
4. *"And what do you know now?"*
5. *"Go back to your original space."*
6. *"And what do you know from here now?"*

Personal Review of Process #3

Write down your experience as the client:

____

____

____

Write down your experience as the facilitator:

____

____

____

And what do you know now?

____

____

____

An Analysis of Process #3

> *I believe anything has to be possible. You have to be able to face any problem that comes along and unravel it into a solution.*
>
> Jon Oringer

An Unravelling

Throughout our lives we make so many choices, have so many choices made for us, have so many defining moments occur, etc. and after all of these and every other twist and turn that a life may take, this all ties up our thinking and understanding about ourselves or a situation into condensed and tangled knots.

This process is designed to unravel these knots, because of this there may be moments during a session where one comes across an old problem or an old structure that had been forgotten all about, this is part of the unravelling and this problem will now in its own way unravel to bring a deep clarity and balance to the person.

Clarity and Balance

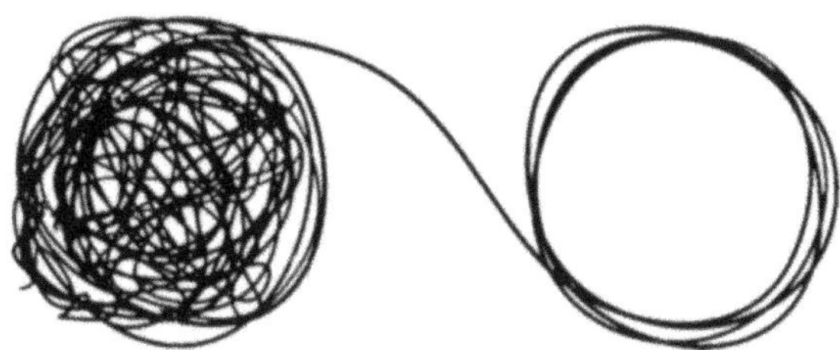

The Unravelling

These terms 'clarity' and 'balance' are excellent references to describe where this process may lead us to. For each intention, each movement and each flow we consider and recognise is a thread in these knots and as we unpick and gently release each one. And through further iterations the revealing and releasing of those underlying threads previously hidden and tightly bound, everything begins to coalesce and take on a new form.

This new form brings a sense of relief and a dissolution of the original problem for the client, allowing them to act and respond in a new and more positive way moving forward.

Process #3 - Example Session (Jean)

Here is a client's session of the Basic Four Flows process. This has been written up afterwards from a recorded session. As this is personal material, any names and references have been changed.

Clean Space work can be difficult to express only in words as so much information is gleaned from the client's interaction with their psychoactive space, where significant adjustments or realisations were made these have been annotated to the transcript.

Thank you to Jean for giving her permission to share this material.

Live Transcript of Process #3

First Iteration (Recognition)

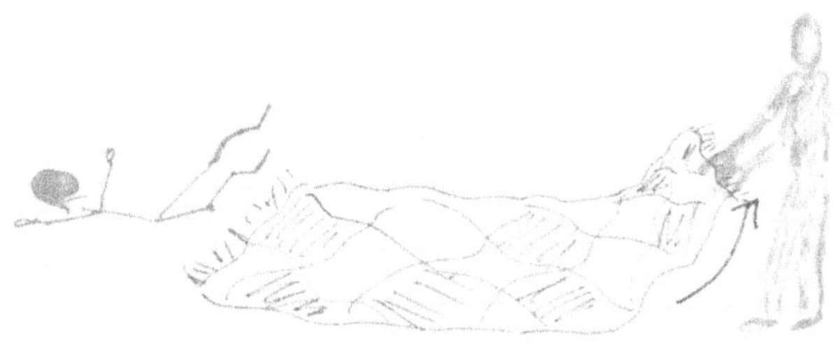

Jean's Starting Piece

"Write up what you'd like to work on."

- The Rug Pull

When Jean came into the session she mentioned that she keeps getting rugs pulled out from beneath her.

"And where are you now in relationship with 'The Rug Pull'?"

- Just back from it, here; this space is called 'Cautious'.

"What must you not get from that?" ('Rug Pull')

- Unpleasantly Surprised.

"What must you get from that?"

- Caution, I'm protecting myself.

"What must you make sure that doesn't get from you?"

- Trust.

"What must you make sure that does get from you?"

- Respectful Ambivalence.

"And what do you know now about this?"

- I constantly get side-swiped by it, I feel it's a semi-regular occurrence in my life.
- This space is called: "It's out to get me!"

Second Iteration (Effect)

We now use "It's out to get me!" as the focus.

"And where are you now in relationship with 'It's out to get me!'?"

- I'm back here, quite a distance away, I'm nowhere near those other bits.

"What must you not get from that?"

- I mustn't allow it to get me, to lull me into a false sense of security, I'm a sucker!

Jean then provides an aside history relating to this false sense of security - It is written down, named "Lewis P." and placed.

"What must you get from that?" (Ref: 'It's out to get me!')

- The Upper Hand as that is the ultimate aim AND not allowing previous rug-pulls to stop me making decisions.

Note that at this point Jean begins to self-model and moving and placing papers herself with no further instruction.

"What must you make sure that doesn't get from you?"

- I suppose it's trust again... It's Implicit Naive Trust - 'cause trusting it is ok, but it's about being aware and not stupid.

"What must you make sure that does get from you?"

- A realistic and understanding relationship with the rug, with an awareness.

"And what do you know now about all of this?"

- I don't have to be frightened of it, I have to teach myself a new way of approaching rugs.
- This space is called: "New Approach"

Third Iteration (System and Form)

We now use "New Approach" as the focus.

"And where are you now in relationship with 'New Approach'?"

- (There were no words here, just a physical movement to a new space)

"What must you not get from that?"

- Over-Enthusiasm because sometimes when I see a new approach I go rushing in. Also recklessness and impatience.

"What must you get from that?"

- A steady direction - a framework for confidence - I see scaffolding in my head like a map... it's a guided map.

"What must you make sure that doesn't get from you?"

- Rushing carelessly through it, it's about balance and not being too heavy on either side.

"What must you make sure that does get from you?"

- Prudence - Looking before you leap! The action of considering the consequences before one acts, this sums up the balance.

"And what do you know now about all of this?"

- It's Achievable!
- This space is called: "It's Achievable!"

Fourth Iteration (Consequences & Contradiction)

We now use “It’s Achievable!” as the focus.

“And where are you now in relationship with ‘It’s Achievable!’?”

- At this point I’ve not started this process yet, so I’m back here... though maybe I’m a bit closer... I would say I’m here because that is me being sober about this and being aware, this is where the speed change begins.

“What must you not get from that?”

- Temptation to rush, that’s what prevents you from looking ahead and this leads to tripping on the rug’s tassels. Which is why I’m face down on the rug and I cannot see the bastard picking up the other end, that’s it! That’s the thing, rushing to the rug, trip up, SPLAT! Thinking “Hello Rug, I’m here I’ve made it!” in the meantime Bastard in stealth mode has come up to the other side to flip me off it!

“What must you get from that?”

- Confidence in the process.

“What must you make sure that doesn’t get from you?”

- Disrespect and impatience - jumping in without any thought, I have to learn there is a process to being in a healthy relationship.

"What must you make sure that does get from you?"

- Respect and patience & diligence to trust and to follow the process and it's pace.

"And what do you know now about all of this?"

- Oooo, I have a tendency towards being impetuous...
- Jean states "This is a bit of a revelation - Let's call it 'Epiphany'"

Fifth Iteration (Unravel)

We now use "Epiphany" as the focus.

"And where are you now in relationship with 'Epiphany'?"

- I'm on the starting blocks, in preparation for the process - "Get Set!"

"What must you not get from that?"

- A false start, hearing the gun before it goes off.

"What must you get from that?"

- A sense of contentment and trust in strength of the starting blocks, the grounding of them. Even though they are temporary they are incredibly strong and grounded for as long as you need them to be.

"What must you make sure that doesn't get from you?"

- That it's not forgotten.

"What must you make sure that does get from you?"

- That it is remembered in the right place - take notice of it in the right place.

"And what do you know now about all of this?"

- To Slow Down, as I've yet to discover what this all is, and that's ok.
- This space is called: "To Slow Down"

Sixth Iteration (Emergence)

We now use "To Slow Down" as the focus.

"And where are you now in relationship with 'To Slow Down'?"

- Here next to the Epiphany, because the Epiphany has the ability to eradicate the old thinking. It is an 'Old-Thinking Eraser'.

"What must you not get from that?"

- Slowing down so much I stop.

"What must you get from that?"

- A healthy pace.

"What must you make sure that doesn't get from you?"

- (laughs) an argument - "You're not going to tell me what to do!"

"What must you make sure that does get from you?"

- A willing cooperation - comes with understanding.

Seventh Iteration (Rest and Consolidation)

Jean is asked to find a space outside all of this, she chooses one near the space "Lewis P." from the second round.

"And what do you know from here?"

- That I can see the WHOLE thing, I've moved to a place where I can get perspective, it's got everything.

"And what else do you know from here?"

- It takes up an awful lot of room, it's quite a spread out thing that takes up a lot of space. It consumes, the old thinking was destructive, whereas actually the new way of thinking might actually take more time it's not going to be a destructive cycle. It's like building the foundations right, so the building doesn't fall down.

"And what else do you know from here?"

- That the rug is actually a lot smaller than I thought it was and it's not as scary.

"And what else do you know from here?"

- Bits are symmetrical, which is not me as I generally don't see symmetry, but this has brought balance. Also, actually the bastard who pulls the rug is actually the same size as me!

"And what else do you know from here?"

- It's quite interesting as in the original drawing I made the rug puller quite solid, whereas I'm just a stick person, like easily blown over, but I don't think that's true. Seeing myself like that is the old way of thinking, I'm not that stick figure anymore.

"And what else do you know from here?"

- Don't go rushing towards the rug, because then I'll be able to see the bastard coming.

Jean is asked to move back to the position she started in.

"And what do you know from here now?"

- That being this close is ridiculous if you want to make a decision. All you're doing is responding to what is in front of your nose. I wouldn't call it cautious now, I think that it is more suffocation, panic and fear - I don't like being here I want to be back over here, this is my space to be [Jean chooses to move back next to 'Lewis P.'], I feel relaxed and I can see everything.

We end the session here with Jean looking at ways of integrating all this information into her day to day activities.

Jean's Feedback

A week later I contact Jean for a catch up she starts off with the following:

"It was an interesting few days after seeing you, I was quite emotional, a little bit wobbly. Uncertain about just stuff, about anything really, about most decisions I was making. That only lasted a couple of days. I was very weepy however, for a good week, it didn't take much to set me off."

Jean then discussed a bit more about what had been happening, she is transitioning between jobs and had been deliberating about if had she made the right decision or not, also there was a great deal of emotional attachment to the people she was working with and was about to leave. All of this was initially expressed with a sense of the old negative emotion attached, it transpired however, that by the end of her story Jean was now talking and perceiving these changes in a different and positive manner, and the changes coming (contract changes) would have previously been seen as a 'rug pull' but not any more. Jean continues:

"I am generally on an upward trajectory emotionally, though I'm still easily provoked to tears. It's different from before, I feel less fortified because I felt my tension was this shield, if I look back on it. I wouldn't have described it like that at the time though. Now I can see that being tense like that has you in that 'fight or flight' readiness state."

"Now it's more like being behind a semi-porous, bendy and pliable membrane that can let things in and out, which before had been uncomfortable and I wouldn't feel or wouldn't let out. So there's things that are coming to me now that I'm feeling, that I wasn't allowing myself to feel from the outside before. There was almost a numbness before, which is beginning to give a little bit, which is quite nice because I feel like I'm beginning to be more like myself, because I wouldn't be numb normally."

"Being ok with not knowing is the point, the thing which pissed me off about the rug being pulled was because I'd put a solid expectation on something being the way that it was, and if it changed I perceived that as a 'rug-pull' and ended up facedown, whereas it doesn't have to be a rug-pull, maybe it's a rug-shift! and that's ok because you can get off, move it across and get back on it again."

"The membrane is flexible, it's breathable, it's not suffocating. My responses now are very different to how they would have been a few weeks ago, things are just rug shifts now. And that bastard is now sat in the corner sucking his thumb, out of a job!" Jean laughs.

Process #4 - The Eternal Moment of Now

"I can see clearly now, the rain is gone,
I can see all obstacles in my way.
Gone are the dark clouds that had me blind.
It's gonna be a bright, bright sun-shiny day."

"I think I can make it now, the pain is gone.
All of the bad feelings have disappeared.
Here is the rainbow, I've been prayin' for.
It's gonna be a bright, bright sun-shiny day."

Johnny Nash - I Can See Clearly Now

We are now about to embark upon Process #4. For reference, this process has been adapted from the Universal Conscious Practice by K.Penday. It was chosen for a couple of reasons.

First, its simplicity and naturally clean approach, which provides people learning the basics of Emergence and Clean Space with a structure to build upon. Secondly, the process has proven to offer noticeable and positive benefits for clients.

Introduction

We will start with looking at the full process structure, and then a live session transcript is provided.

Just as Process #1 is beautiful in its simplicity, so is Process #4. For a quick overview, we can briefly express the steps of Process #4 as:

1. Describe now
2. Locate a past
3. Compare to now
4. Locate a future
5. Compare to now
6. Repeat two more times from #2
7. Repeat five more times from #1

The process has the client repetitively locating past and future memories/ideas and comparing these to their current 'Now' state each time. After six such comparisons, a new 'Now' is recoginised and the process repeats.

The following page provides the utilised definitions to make sure the client and the facilitator fully understand the process, then follows a full explanation of the process and its implementation.

Utilised Definitions

These are the appropriate definitions of the main words utilised in this process, these may be used if there are any misunderstandings about the questions used.

Where (could be any of these)

- In or to what situation, state or condition
- A place or viewpoint
- An identity or attitude
- A mood or emotion

Might

- Used to express possibility

Compare

- Note the similarity and dissimilarity between

Process #4 Step by Step

Step 1 - Now

To begin, ask your client,

"And, where are you now?"

It has sometimes been noticed that on first running this process with some clients their initial understanding of this question is to give a location. Acknowledge this, and follow up using a precursor such as:

"Okay, and in life, where are you now?"

This is a Stage 1 (Recognition) question and therefore comes with the Download and Upload features, so the client will initially be answering verbally and once they have fully expressed themselves, they should now represent (by writing or drawing) their answer on paper.

Once all the information has been represented, you will need to direct the client into placing that paper somewhere in space, as discussed in the section on Navigation.

Step 2 - Past

The next step is bringing the client's attention into their past. Here we use the question:

"And, where have you been?"

Depending on the clients experience with the process, you could use:

- *"And in the past, where have you been?"* or
- *"And before now, where have you been?"* or
- *"And earlier in life, where have you been?"*

Following the same 'Download and Upload' procedure as above, have them verbalise and then represent their answer on paper. This could be on the same sheet(s) or a new sheet. Let the client decide. If they ask you what to do, you can reply,

"And, where does that belong?"

whilst gesturing openly towards the existing paper(s) and space.

If the client has chosen a new sheet, once it has been completed, you will need to direct the client into placing that paper in relationship to the first paper placed. Use the direction:

"And, place that where it belongs in relation to where you are now."

indicating towards the first sheet, or

"And, place that where it belongs in relation to all of this."

gesturing across the emerging client's landscape.

Step 3 - Compare

The client now has two representations ('the past' and 'now'), we are going to have the client notice the differences and similarities between these two responses.

Ask,

"And compare that to where you are now."

indicating for the client which information you are referring to as you say it. So you would gently gesture towards the information/paper for the past, and then the information/paper for now.

You may choose to exchange 'where you have been' for 'that' in the question, for example,

"And compare where you have been to where you are now."

This addition to the instruction has limited value and has been found to be best utilised only in the first few iterations - then falling back to the original usage of 'that' later on.

Any new information that emerges in this stage should also be written down. The client may choose to do this on either the existing sheets or on a new sheet or sheets altogether.

> For each new sheet of paper, follow the above procedure and have the client place it in a space where it belongs in relationship to the other sheet(s). As this technique will become the norm throughout the process, there is no need for us to keep repeating this in each step going forward.

Note that once the client has more than one piece (sheet) of information in their space and they are now considering the relating spatial relationships between them, it can happen that existing sheets have to move their existing position(s) to accommodate the new emerging information.

Allow the client the time and space to reorganise their world. This is the moment that the space becomes psychoactive for the client. Remember, do not interfere with this process, do not offer 'friendly' assistance or your own inferences about where or what the placement of the papers means.

Step 4 - Future

Now we are looking to take the client's attention towards their future. This step is run exactly the same as Step 2, however, the question asked is:

"And, where might you be?"

Alternatives could be:

- *"And later in life, where might you be?"*

or

- *"And in the future, where might you be?"*

Step 5 - Compare

This is virtually exactly the same as Step 3; however, have the client compare the future space to the present space by directing them with:

- *"And compare that to where you are now."*

or

- *"And compare where you might be to where you are now."*

Step 6 - Reiterate

We now have, spoken then represented by the client, where they are now (present), where they have been in the past, and where they might be in the future, along with any further information gleaned from the two comparisons.

We will now reiterate Steps 2 through to 5 until the client has explored and compared three past spaces and three future spaces. The image below gives a visual representation of how this step of the process runs.

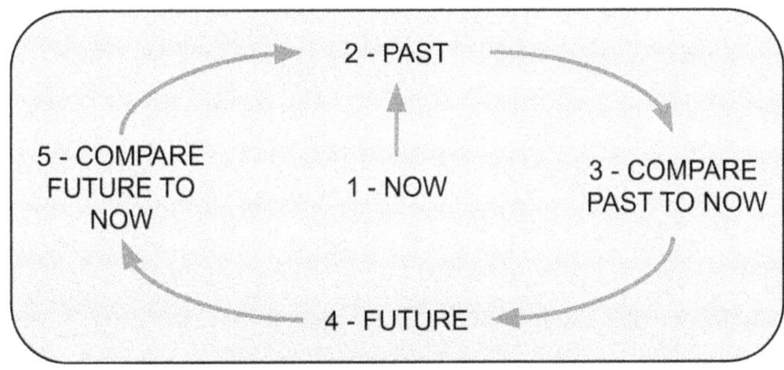

Reiteration of Steps 2 to 5

For the instructions given in these repeated steps, the word 'else' may be utilised to confirm for the client that a 'new' event or moment in time is required.

It has been known for some clients to continue to focus on the same future and past spaces or very similar alternatives. This, however, is simply part of the process; allow them to go through this. The use of 'else' aims to help take their attention to other times and spaces.

- *"And, where else have you been?"*
- *"And, where else might you be?"*

When asking for *"Where else might you be?"* clients are being given the opportunity to look in their own way at all the possibilities and choices available to them. The facilitator and process are not advocating or dismissing the potential successes or failures of the client - this is up to them.

Step 7 - Continue the Reiteration

We are now going to repeat Steps 1 through to 6 this is generally repeated another five times. On each new full round, it is recommended to restart with a new sheet of paper and have the previous 'Now' sheet placed where it belongs in relationship with everything else, before beginning the new moment of 'Now', if it has not already been placed.

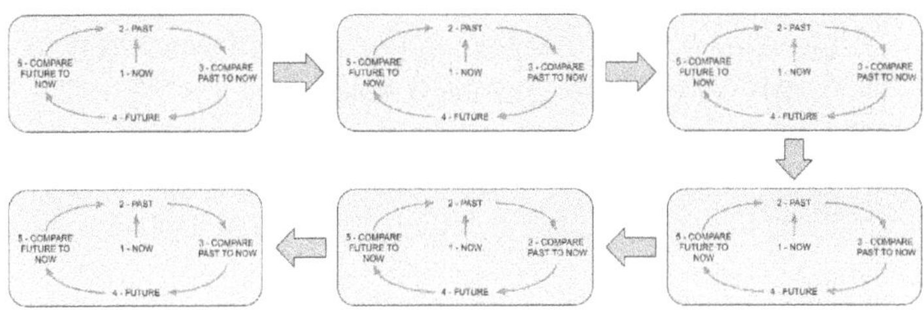

Six Iterations of Step 6

Running six sets of Steps 1 to 6 is not a hard and fast rule. If the client comes to a new deeper understanding - such as suddenly realising how all their previously unrelated past and future moments are all connected - or they suddenly realise that they're (stated with a resounding "I" or "Me") now very much in the room with you in the 'Here and Now', accompanied with a big smile and sense of relief, then the session may move straight to the next step.

Step 8 - Finishing Off

The finishing questions of the session are:

"And, what do you know now?"

Then,

"And, what is the difference between what you knew at the beginning and what you know now?"

And finally,

"And, knowing that, what difference does that make?"

Summary of Process #4

Have the client verbalise and represent on paper the answers to each step below. These papers, once created, are placed in the space around the client in relationship to everything else.

A single round of the process looks like this, where after each question or instruction the client represents their response:

- *"And, where are you now?"*
- *"And, where have you been?"*
- *"And, compare that to where you are now"*
- *"And, where might you be?"*
- *"And, compare that to where you are now"*
- *"And, where else have you been?"*
- *"And, compare that to where you are now"*
- *"And, where else might you be?"*
- *"And, compare that to where you are now"*
- *"And, where else have you been?"*
- *"And, compare that to where you are now"*
- *"And, where else might you be?"*
- *"And, compare that to where you are now"*

This structure is then repeated until the client experiences the 'Here and Now', or a recognition of a positive shift of understanding about their life occurs. This generally occurs on the sixth iteration, but not always. If you're required to maintain a time limit to the session, then six iterations is recommended.

Finally, ask the finishing questions,

- *"And, what do you know now?"*
- *"And, what is the difference between what you knew at the beginning and what you know now?"*
- *"And, knowing that, what difference does that make?"*

Personal Review of Process #4

Write down your experience as the client:

____

____

____

Write down your experience as the facilitator:

____

____

____

And what do you know now?

____

____

____

An Analysis of Process #4

> *"You cannot suffer the past or future because they do not exist. What you are suffering is your memory and your imagination."*
>
> Sadhguru

Simplicity Itself

Throughout this process, the client explores what is happening in the here and now, by iteratively focusing their attention on prior and future constructs. Through this, we begin to separate what is actually happening now, and what is been created by the client about their past or their future in the here and now.

The end product of the process is when the client comes to a new understanding of their life and they are fully present in the room with you. This also beneficially recovers their lost attention units that were previously allocated to stuck ideas or thoughts about their life.

A Very Clean Start

Our starting question, *"And, where are you now?"*, offers the client a way to express themselves with the potential for some evaluation of their life up to the here and now.

Things that may be considered and voiced by the client are:

- What it is that brought them to this moment
- Where they are heading
- What their problem is
- What their purpose in life is
- How they are not getting what they want
- What they do not like about themselves

The question *"And, where are you now?"* is chosen to purposefully not request an intention, not to propose a goal or an ambition, not to suppose the client is wrong or broken in any way. It is simply to discover where they are in their life at this moment. If they choose to go delving any deeper, that is their choice.

Spotting Differences and Similarities

The level of our ability to recognise differences between what we are experiencing is directly proportional to the depth of what we, as individuals, are capable of experiencing. That may seem an obvious statement at first reading, but it does have far-reaching consequences, and those consequences are within our control, if we choose to adapt and become cognizant of our own experience of life.

For instance, the extent of our vocabulary provides us with the communicating power to express ourselves to the extent that our vocabulary allows. If we do not have the words and the psychological structures of particular concepts, we are unable to fully comprehend and attend to various experiences.

Examples of this are those people whom have studied and gained a knowledge of music, art, craftsmanship, architecture, etc. Their experience of a particular related item and that of another person without a similar level of understanding, will be very different - the aspects of appreciation will be different.

I often make the point, when training NLP and EK, that one of the purposes of the training and learning of the models is that as we become more and more aware of our inner structures our self-awareness or the intelligence of ourselves increases, thus offering us more control in life.

We are teaching ourselves the finer and finer distinctions we have about our life and human connectivity. The fewer distinctions we have, the more everything is the same, and our ability to make valued and effective judgements is impeded.

It is for all the above reasons, that this process purposefully includes the step to compare where the client is now and where they might be or have been, we call this 'Splitting Time'. This comparison has the client bring their attention to what is actually different and similar between these two independent constructs.

As a facilitator, it is very interesting to take a mental note of the categories of similarity and differences proposed by the client - especially for later more advanced Emergent processes.

During the 'Comparison' step, the facilitator may specifically request similarities and differences, especially if differences are not forthcoming. Sometimes clients in 'stuck' problem situations are unable to spot them.

Being unable to Split Time, through the use of spotting differences, may have the client continuing to have parts of their historical record connecting to, and thus occurring, in the present moment.

Spotting new similarities and differences is key to success in this process.

More on Splitting Time

Splitting Time is where the things (e.g. events, ideas, incidents) which are not here and now are looked at and checked against the here and now. Doing this provides the client an opportunity to disconnect these structures. This splits apart these (defining) moments for the client, and has them re-placing these prior or future events back to where they belong or come from.

If there are moments in the client's past, or potential future, which they are uncomfortable viewing, they are in control of choosing to go or not go there. Later on they may find themselves taking a peek and, through multiple iterations of viewing over time, they may come to a new understanding of these events and, finally, view them in their entirety with no ill effects.

And at some point, as an added bonus, the client may also come to realise that all the things they have been worrying about are no longer an actual present time reality, and have, unfortunately, just been unconsciously getting created by themselves in the here and now! This can be quite a revelation when directly experienced, and is even more powerful once they notice and decide to stop doing it.

A Little Troubleshooting

It is worth recognising that in the beginning some clients will only look at generalised times in their past or future. If this is becoming a pattern, and no progress is being made, you can ask,

"And, what is your first memory connected to that?" or,

"And when have you had that before?"

This approach may also be utilised if the client suddenly begins to express emotions, ideas or thoughts that were not there in the beginning.

Having a client access specific memories has been shown to offer a deeper experience. The details provided of such a memory would have some or all of the following conditions:

- Having a specific time and place
- Who was there
- What happened
- How long that particular episode lasted
- The actions and choices made in that moment
- The emotions, ideas and thoughts associated

There is an interesting reference here to David and his follow up questions especially when dealing with the Iterative Pattern of Sixes, for after asking for the First Memory, he would follow up with asking for the Second, Third, Fourth, Fifth and then Sixth. Though, this iterative pattern is not currently recommended whilst running this process.

Process #4 - Example Session (Mark)

Here follows a client's session. I am very grateful to Mark for offering this material to share, as this session covers some very deep and personal material. All names and references have been changed.

This is an extensive transcript, it is included in its entirety to provide a real model for understanding some of the information and ideas that may evolve from what appears at first glance to be a very simple emergent process.

Live Transcript of Process #4

First Iteration (Recognition)

And, where are you now?

- Looking for a new life. I've grown sick of working the same jobs, and now want to do something that actually satisfies me, and isn't just something that earns money and keeps me in the rat-race.

And, where have you been?

- At my desk answering the phone, sending out quotes, following them up - selling someone else's products to make them money.

Compare where you have been to where you are now

- Well, at the time I was happy enough doing it for what I was paid. But now it's very different. It doesn't satisfy me any more, even in the money.

And, where might you be?

- Doing something I really love doing. That does open up a few options though! Ermm.. having a thriving base of clients using my NLP skills.

Compare where you might be to where you are now

- That is a new life, happy - where I was hoping or planning to be - the sick feeling has gone, I look back on the old job.

And, where else have you been?

- Just finishing college, I was free for a while - doing what I wanted, seemed like there wasn't any responsibility at that time, just a time to enjoy.

Compare where you have been to where you are now

- Worlds apart. Now I'm stuck in a whole host of responsibility and it's the kind I'm not happy with - back then was so easy.

And, where else might you be?

- Still stuck in this job, doing the same thing - earning money, but the longer I'm in it, the more I want to get out. So I'll be on a spiral of depression.

Compare where you might be to where you are now

- This is like my fear, somewhere I don't want to go - I've had a breakdown already, I don't want another one - at the moment I have a choice and that is good!

And, where else have you been?

- I had a choice when going to University, when leaving University and after college - it seems like the number of choices get smaller as I get older... is that what this is actually about?

Compare where you have been to where you are now

- I'm at a point when I don't feel like I have many choices left. It's like if I stay I'm stuffed and if I leave then I'm stepping into the unknown and I don't know if I will survive.

And, where else might you be?

- I could be on the phone, talking to the ex-boss, pleading for my job back… but at least I'd tried something new or different.

Compare where you might be to where you are now

- I'd be a step forward - at least I would know the result. In this situation it is a failed attempt, but the recovery is doable - I think. What else would happen if the ex-boss said no…?

Second Iteration (Effect)

And, where are you now?

- What is my worth? Do this company actually value me? Do I value myself? What am I willing to do to provide for my wellbeing and that of my family?

And, where have you been?

- My lowest point was probably when everything went wrong with Melanie. I went off the rails a bit - strayed from the path and got myself into trouble - that led to another real low, to get out that place... Damn, it feels like I never really recovered, I still dread some of the thoughts from then.

Compare where you have been to where you are now

- I have built myself up to now, I got through all of that - yes, parts still affect me, they probably always will - it's like that story of the ball in a box pressing a button - Now I want to take myself to the next stage, it's as though I've had enough suffering, it's time for something good to really happen.

And, where might you be?

- I could be living in a place like Spain or France, not too far from what is happening back home with the family, but somewhere where I am comfortable - not sure how I am supporting myself here, but I'm happy drinking red wine, eating cheese and fresh baked bread.

Compare where you might be to where you are now

- 'Now' is very serious - 'Then' is that freedom I had - freedom from all the stresses from now - it's a pipedream. A lovely, long extended holiday - a retirement plan..? Why wait till you're nearly dead in the ground to enjoy all the things you've worked your life for..?

And, where else have you been?

- At eight years old, sat in a library - fascinated with all the books and information around me.

Compare where you have been to where you are now

- Very different - there doesn't seem to be a sense of value for me, the value then was on the vast stores of knowledge around me - now it is about having something else value me... I valued it (books etc.), now it (work, company, myself) has to value me... what the fuck?

And, where else might you be?

- I could be still in the first 'Now' place, wondering, hoping, deliberating over and over and never getting anywhere.

Compare where you might be to where you are now

- That would be stepping back, feels like I've already moved on - I could be deliberating over values, wondering what is important? That's what I am wondering now, and to who is the importance aligned with? For me, for someone or something else?

And, where else have you been?

- Completing my NLP course, excited and euphoric about doing something amazing with it all.

Compare where you have been to where you are now

- There is a sense of what I can do in the world now. I am offering value at another level than just selling stuff. Now I am doubting or questioning my value. Have I lost my way?

And, where else might you be?

- With a firm acknowledgment of value for self and what is being done - knowing that I am on the right path - like confirmation of doing my life's work. Walking a path that was designed? or laid out for me? but that goes against my sense of choice and will... maybe it is something else.. not defined... something else...

Compare where you might be to where you are now

- The company doesn't exist in the future one - It is me and my focus, doing something with dedication and motivation - very different from the query and questioning of now.

Third Iteration (System and Form)

And, where are you now?

- Looking at how all this could come about - thinking that I need a plan, a way to achieve what I really want - but that is what is needed first: a firm idea of what I want to be.

And, where have you been?

- At an old job, took what was available, I needed to earn some cash so took it - they were ok to work for, but eventually I began to see they were abusing my position by getting more and more from me but not paying for it. I left then.

Compare where you have been to where you are now

- I realised that I was worth more than what they were paying - these people will do that and keep doing that unless you prove that you're worth more to them. Leaving is not the only option. I had an option then, another one came along... if that had not been there would I have continued on in despair? Did I create the opportunity? In that the new company recognised I was worth more, then yes!

And, where might you be?

- Having someone recognise I am worth more - so that I don't take responsibility for the change, they are the catalyst - there is something unsettling about that... I should be the one to create change.

Compare where you might be to where you are now

- Having an option put in front of me, now is looking for one, not creating one, now I am considering that if I do not have that plan or idea, then all that will happen is I will require an option placed in front of me - in that way it is a basic choice: stay or go.

And, where else have you been?

- Empowering myself through further education, so that more opportunities were available to me.

Compare where you have been to where you are now

- I had a plan of the kind of work I wanted to be doing, so I paid and trained in it - that was also true of the NLP work, I thought it was just for interest, but then it became something more valuable than that - the potential was greater - maybe I need to train more?

And, where else might you be?

- On another course - maybe a trainers course or another method, maybe learning EK or Clean better?

Compare where you might be to where you are now

- Later there is an intention, something to move towards - but is it just short term? The ideas of now are longer term, maybe I am not pushing my timeline forward enough - I'm stuck here and cannot see there...

And, where else have you been?

- Getting the job at the desk, that appeared to fit all the criteria - security, big name, fresh start, safe. But boring, damn boring, and the policy and backstabbing to climb the ladder is appalling. This is not what I signed up for and if I keep my head down and just do this I'll end up brain-dead. But getting the job was a great feeling, full of aspiration... so what happened?

Compare where you have been to where you are now

- Some of the key factors, like aspiration with security and that safe feeling - that has gone. Now it's just monotonous - Am I looking for a 'bazinga', 'bang', 'woo-woo' kind of thing? or just something that I can mould into my own creation? I started here thinking that working for another was a no-no and that keeps coming back to mind.

And, where else might you be?

- I can assist with some training courses, I've got the connections - They would probably be unpaid, but I would get to help out, I would get additional training and some great experience with new learners - and maybe even get to apply that extra knowledge at my current role.

Compare where you might be to where you are now

- This is a far more positive stance - there is a half-way house, it's not all out or all in - this has a good feeling attached.

Fourth Iteration (Consequences and Contradiction)

And, where are you now?

- Now thinking of possibilities, some real, down to earth actions that can actually happen - there is also a shift in how I feel about work, as if I can do something about it now.

And, where have you been?

- Making the firm decision to leave my role at the time, handing over my letter of resignation.

Compare where you have been to where you are now

- Back then I had confirmation in what I was about to do. There was a set future in place, I'd kind of made the necessary connections and had a viable plan. It worked out for a short time.

And, where might you be?

- There's a moment where I am leading some training sessions, I am clearly delivering content and also training clients on the models and techniques.

Compare where you might be to where you are now

- There is more similarity here - feels like a reality, something that is achievable - feels like my unconscious is already putting plans in place.

And, where else have you been?

- The alternative is here, when the plan never worked - I went back to a job that was shit and was expecting it to be different. I had to claim 'depression' and being overwhelmed, I had to get out - interestingly that started me on a clearer path, one that I was building. Not one put down by the organisation that I was working for.

Compare where you have been to where you are now

- There's a sense that this new place I could go to, would be similar - it would be my land. Am I brave enough to do it, am I prepared?

And, where else might you be?

- Stuck, questioning, on the street - I lose my house and family, I am unable to support anyone, even myself - this is like the worst situation that could occur - I suppose I have to consider it...

Compare where you might be to where you are now

- It could happen, this is a reality for some people - when everything lines up and it all goes wrong, I don't feel I would go that destitute, I'm not an alcoholic, or drug addict, my dependencies are the kids - If it all went to shit, I would get a job picking potatoes if I had to.

And, where else have you been?

- What's the shittest thing I've had to do? ... The worst experience was the abuse - not by choice, but it was the worst thing that happened.

Compare where you have been to where you are now

- There were no possibilities, the only thing I could do was lock it all up, put on a brave face and pretend to everyone that nothing was wrong - I was scared to let people know, as it would be my fault and my parents would want to know what I had done to make it happen... That was my thinking, it was a sad situation and still today, no one knows about it. Now there are possibilities, but they are tainted by this. That same idea of "it's all my fault, what have I done?"

And, where else might you be?

- I could be stuck continuing to express this inner fear, to be self-blaming and not doing things because of a deep rooted pain.

Compare where you might be to where you are now

- Are these the same? There was a feeling of positivity, now it's anything but that. The bit that they are both possible realities, if this pain remains then will I always hold this fear and being scared to move - one of them is me now and the other is twelve - a twelve year old who is wracked with guilt and fear.

Fifth Iteration (Unravel)

And, where are you now?

- I don't know any more - at one point I was happy about this and now I'm confused and upset, I wasn't expecting to have those memories come back. I'd locked them away. To see that they are still affecting me is sad and also frustrating. That young me was lost and no one could help, as they didn't know. I was so very introverted, I have always been so very introverted since then, in fact I think I probably still am - that's why I keep going round in circles with all this. I keep it all inside

And, where have you been?

- Coming home after the first time it happened, I was quiet and said everything was ok. Then went upstairs to the bathroom to clean myself, then there is nothing.

Compare where you have been to where you are now

- That is a blank, I know that there is sadness and guilt, trying and willing it all to go away. I didn't know what to do then, too. I went into hiding, learning to put on a brave face, to not have any feeling, whilst enveloped in some inner turmoil. That turmoil is still there - that is where this comes from. From a scared, confused and upset child with no voice or ally to be with. I feel now like I'm all on my own with this, feel that no one else can understand what is happening, so I keep it all inside.

And, where might you be?

- Sitting comfortable with all the above, after resolving all the issues - knowing that the pain and hurt from those yesterdays no longer have to cause me problems in today. Seeing the connections of those feelings and how I was being exposed, in what is happening now and has been happening to me, and knowing that they no longer need to do that, that those things have passed and I have grown older and it may take time but it is possible for the past to be cleared and for it to be eventually laid to rest.

Compare where you might be to where you are now

- Acceptance versus confusion, a brighter future versus a stuck past, a new idea about me and what I can be - in a way who I am already becoming... strange!?!

And, where else have you been?

- I got an image of me as a baby, innocent and calm.

Compare where you have been to where you are now

- The now is a little different, it's not the innocent and calm - that's like a vast open future - infinite possibilities but with no required intention. The now I have is not as confused, a bit more relaxed, a bit more accepting of who I have been and become. There is intention and direction now. It feels like I can reach out. Before, I was reaching in.

And, where else might you be?

- There's a large room with banners and rows and rows of people, I'm there as a guest speaker, looking smart and professional - everyone looks interested and cheerful. There is acceptance within me and towards me. I haven't seen this or felt this before, there doesn't feel to be anything getting in the way.

Compare where you might be to where you are now

- It is like now and my feelings are coming together, what I am experiencing is actually happening within me - even though this is a possible future, it is like I am creating it without effort.

And, where else have you been?

- It is the baby again, with a smile, like the baby is creating and just being there, enjoying life and the love bestowed upon it - pure joy.

Compare where you have been to where you are now

- I would like some of that joy, that positive easy feeling riding over me, with nothing to get in the way, nothing to stop how I feel or how I may express myself, my ideas and thoughts just happen - like sparks and my body is alive, my mind is lighting up.

And, where else might you be?

- I'm just here, right now - this is wonderful, it feels like I came full circle or something. Wow, I am right here.

Compare where you might be to where you are now

- This is now (laughs).

Sixth Iteration (Emergence)

The sixth iteration was not required as the client was experiencing the expected end result of the process.

The finishing off questions followed.

Finishing Off

And, what do you know now?

- That my history had held me back, that I was caught up in quite a tangled mess - there are lots of things to do, especially with work and stuff but that doesn't actually feel like it is or even was the problem. I'd like to enjoy this feeling some more.

The next two standard questions were dropped as the client was enjoying the moment, so I finished off with a simple:

And, is there anything else you would like to share?

- No, just thank you! Thank you.

THE FUTURE

- Moving On
- Emergence

Moving On

> "You cannot step in the same river twice."
>
> Heraclitus

Now you have some experience of using Clean Space and the Iterative Patterns of Emergence through these processes, you will be beginning to develop a connection to your internal navigator. You may now be wondering what happens next?

New Processes and the Future

Many other Emergent processes have been developed over the intervening years. My work with David was based on breaking down each stage of an EK process into a specific unit. This has now provided us with a collection of units, which it is possible to connect together in an infinite variety of ways. The benefit of this is that new processes may be designed and expressed using this terminology.

As well as the original processes, a selection of new Emergent approaches have been developed by myself. Some of these can be experienced on the Powers of Six website, others are delivered in training courses and will also be presented in the follow-up book in the near future.

More processes from The Holigral Method may initially be discovered from Pam's book, "The Emperor's New Psychology". For more details on training or facilitation in this method, please contact Pam direct through her website: http://www.holigral.com

I have presented another of Pam's original processes, 'The Issue Buster', on the Powers of Six website where it can be experienced in full using the online Iterator. Other notable processes Pam has developed are: The Space In-Between, Re-Scaling, Story-Busting and Pronoun-Scaling.

As more research occurs, new ideas and techniques are being developed. This is a vibrant field with a vast scope of growth and evolution available.

You are very welcome

to join us on this adventure

Contact Matthew by email on

matthew@self-alignment.com

Process #5 - The ABC World

Well done you made it this far!

Here's a little extra for you:

1. "What would you like to focus on this session?"
2. "Position yourself where are you now in relationship to that."
3. "And what (else) do you know about that from here?" x 6
4. "And what do you know now?"
5. "Move to a different space"
6. "And what (else) does that know about you from there?" x 6
7. "And what do you know now?"
8. "Move to a different space"
9. "And what (else) is in between you and that?" x 6
10. "And what do you know now?"
11. "Move to a different space"
12. "And what (else) do you know about that from here?" x 6
13. "And what do you know now?"
14. "Move to a different space"
15. "And what (else) does that know about you from there?" x 6

16. "And what do you know now?"
17. "Move to a different space"
18. "And is there anything else about all of this?" x 6
19. "And what do you know now?"
20. "Move to where you were when you started"
21. "And what do you know from here now?"
22. "And what is the difference between what you know now and when you started?"

Emergence

Back when I was young
Parts of me still hang
A future path, undefined
Those parts still
        frozen in time

Then brought to the fore
To the here and now
Experienced again
Re-wound

Now shaken & stirred
   upset & confused
The growing up again has just begun
Old feelings, words and states of mind
Are felt
   then blow away

Did we hold on to remember?
To relinquish control?
To be safe and secure in a cruel world?

Now

Stepping out into sunshine
Blue skies and change
These old baby eyes are renewed
To see a new world
Experienced again
"Don't take it away!"

... and release ...

It's only a passing phase
As the young fills its space
on the inside

To grow and be whole
To be in the world
And the fear is not here at all

Matthew Hudson - 22 June 2008

APPENDICES

1. Further Resources
2. Seven Days
3. A Set of Brief Histories

Appendix 1 - Further Resources

Clean Language

Books

- 'Metaphors in Mind' by James Lawley and Penny Tompkins
- 'Clean Language' by Wendy Sullivan and Judy Rees
- 'From Contempt to Curiosity' by Caitlin Walker
- 'Resolving Traumatic Memories' by David Grove and Basil Panzer
- 'Trust Me, I'm the Patient' by Philip Harland

Websites

- www.cleanlanguage.co.uk
- www.cleanlearning.co.uk
- www.trainingattention.co.uk
- www.wayfinderpress.com

Emergent Knowledge and Clean Space

e-Books

- Both available from www.self-alignment.com
  - 'Journeys with Emergent Knowledge' and
  - 'Self-Alignment' by Matthew Hudson

Books

- 'The Emperor's New Psychology' by Steven Saunders
- 'Insights in Space' by Marian Way and James Lawley
- 'The Power of Six' by Philip Harland

Websites

- www.powersofsix.com
- www.self-alignment.com/dokuwiki
- www.holigral.com

Videos

- Series of YouTube videos on EK - Audio Recording of David Grove, videos created by Matthew Hudson
  - goo.gl/YVrNmQ
- A complete Clean Space demo by James Lawley
  - vimeo.com/355804386

Appendix 2 - Seven Days

Stages of Emergence and The Days of Week

Here is presented a very interesting insight from Pam Saunders in how the pattern of Six [+1] relates to what we in the Occident have all inherited through our culture and ancestors – the seven day week.

The clues to this ancient pattern are still encased within the original names and symbolism of the days of the week:

- Sunday – The day of the Sun
  - Represents the self, one's personality and ego. It is our identity and our face to the world. The space of 'A'.
- Monday – The day of the Moon
  - Represents the unconscious, feelings and emotions – this is the reflected self. The space of 'B'.
- Tuesday – Tiw's day, the day of Mars
  - The god of war and agriculture. Representing the space of 'C'; where the war / growth between A and B takes place.
- Wednesday – Woden's day, the day of Mercury
  - Woden/Odin held the power to bind or unbind a man's mind. This is the midpoint of the pattern and interestingly Odin is traditionally depicted

with a raven on each shoulder and a wolf on either side of him, representing balance. Mercury is the "messenger of the Gods", the hermaphroditic intermediary between the Sun (A) and the Moon (B).

- Thursday – Thor's day, the day of Jupiter.
  - Thor, the God of thunder, whose hammer is able to throw lightning bolts. Jupiter astrologically represents the ability of the organism and the spirit to expand, and in Roman mythology also has the symbol of a lightning bolt and is the King of the Gods, bringing truth and intellect. The opening of 'C' and a bolt from 'D'
- Friday – Freya's day, the day of Venus
  - The goddess of love, beauty, and fertility. Bringing into being, manifestation. The emergence of a new creation 'E'.
- Saturday – The day of Saturn
  - Signifying rest and contemplation. Saturn also represents our limitations, our restrictions, yet he is also our inner mentor and teacher. His lessons are manifested only over time, after which we go through inner rebirth and enjoy spiritual growth. The integration of 'E' -> 'A'.

This connection between the two patterns (the naming and order of the days with the seven stages of emergence) opens the door to many questions and for myself conjures up many interesting ideas about how this could be so.

In my mind there is no doubt that the pattern matches, my query is based on the historical record and to this I am unable to give an answer. So I simply offer this here now as a curiosity - dwell upon the significance in your own manner and time, I am very happy to hear and learn of your considerations in this matter.

Pam's description is linked more closely to engineering process and to the essential nature of the fractal, such as cycle, projection, reflection, space, metaphor, sequence and manifesting. See "The Emperor's New Psychology" for a full exploration of this.

I have further researched this patterning for interest and discovered that this structure, the days of the weeks and their symbolism, reaches back as far as the Sumerians. From there this pattern then echoes out through the Egyptian, Greek, Roman and Germanic cultures.

Appendix 3 - A Set of Brief Histories

As stated in the beginning my understanding and experience of EK would not be what it is without the open and generous gifts given to me from David and Pam. Here follows a brief outline of their histories and the time they spent together. Over the years many people have had an influence on the development of EK, it appears this was David's way, he would connect with others and cybernetically transfer the learning from outside professions into the work he was doing at the time.

My focus on Pam and her developments in this book is due to our close connection and the work we have done together. I do not intend this piece to infer that others were not also contributing to David's understanding and development of EK, for this is not the case. James Lawley and Penny Tompkins, Shaun Hotchkiss, Cei Davies Linn, Caitlin Walker, Carol Wilson, John Farrell, Philip Harland, Steven Briggs, Bill Rawlin are only some of the names that have also had a direct influence, my apologies if I have missed any names of notable importance.

Following these brief histories is my short memoir from meeting David up to the present time (2019).

Histories

David Grove

"A gentle genie has escaped from the lamp. His name is David Grove and his magic, Clean Language."
Ernest Rossi

David was born in New Zealand of Maori and European ancestry. He graduated in zoology at the University of Canterbury in 1972, and gained an MBA from Otago University in 1973. His professional development as a counselling psychologist included a degree in Counselling from the State University of Minnesota and a study of Ericksonian Hypnosis and a short encounter with NLP.

In the 1980's he developed Clean Language as a response to clients' subjective experiences of phobias and trauma.

This methodology is a set of simple, yet powerful questions that help clients fully explore and develop their personal metaphors for their experience. As the client develops and learns more about their metaphoric world(s), the metaphor typically begins to modify of its own accord, resulting in the relief or resolution of the problem. This was David's initial creation and set him up to become one of the world's most innovative therapists.

He and Cei, David's wife at the time, continued to evolve and develop their ideas in their Healing the Wounded Child Within programme and Therapeutic Metaphor work. This then culminated in a revolutionary shift in his approach, David began to have the client utilise the space around them and explore their relationship to it. It was here that he further developed the patterning of sixes, discovered by Bill Rawlin (David's mentor), that would eventually become the foundation of Emergent Knowledge.

David travelled the world sharing his work with thousands of therapists and those interested in change work, who in turn after falling in love with Clean Language and this idea or philosophy of Clean, began to share and train the material themselves.

Pam Saunders

"It may be twenty or thirty years before the world is ready for what you know."
David Grove

Pam is a chartered engineer and a physicist. In her earlier life she'd worked on developing military radar systems for the UK Government, though by 2003 she had moved out of this field and had begun her own research and developments into the human mind, trauma and the nature of association and dissociation. This was the same set of ideas and questions that David was asking and working on at the time and therefore became the catalyst for bringing David and Pam to work together.

This happened in July 2005 when Steven was hosting his second Integral NLP Conference, which included several

Clean Language presenters. Although David was not presenting he was in attendance. Here began what was to be 18 months of collaboration and development work together.

David continued working and presenting with other people during this period - see the Clean Language website for articles and information on his other collaborations - his close collaboration with Steven was in continuing to develop the principles and processes of Emergent Knowledge.

An Emergent Collaboration

David was now living and working from Steven and Josie's home in Glastonbury, their collaboration and co-developments at this time furthered the development of Emergent Knowledge, such as recognising that the emergent patterns were fractal in nature, and recognising that David's existing Clean Space work actually operated in all 3D planes, this sparked a chain of events and developments to bring the use of the 'Whirly-Gig' for therapeutic interventions into being.

The 'Whirly-Gig' is a large three-ringed device with a harnessed seat positioned in the centre ring. The rings are connected together with full 360 degree rotational pivot points. Which allows the person sat in the seat to completely move in all 3 dimensions. This is all controlled by a facilitator and an assistant moving and supporting the rings by hand.

David was using this machine to aid the client in reclaiming and accessing memories of their prior defining moments. There is a significant amount of technical information around how and why the 'Whiry-Gig' achieves this, though I will only summarise here that the use of the machine provides a mechanism that may begin to align the client to the original spatial positioning and measurement of their moment of trauma.

David facilitating a client on the Whirly-Gig (France 2007)

David's theory of dissociation states that an aspect of self (The Wounded Child) metaphorically leaves the body and is transferred into the locus of where the client's attention was at the time of the trauma. Re-aligning the client to the same direction, azimuth and body position in the present time aids in re-opening this 'portal' for the recovery of this aspect, it is said that this aspect had become 'frozen in time'. This is termed 'Explosive fragmentation'. There is also 'Implosive fragmentation', where the attention goes inside a body part.

In December 2006 the collaboration between David and Steven broke down and they separated ways. Steven continued to work on developing his own processes and theoretical models now known as 'The Holigral Method', David focused on defining and developing the core principles of Emergent Knowledge along with his own set of processes.

Memoir

My Connection with David and Pam

Around the same time of this separation, I had begun furthering my own training and development in NLP on my Masters course in Newcastle. It was here I was introduced to Clean Language by Caitlin Walker. I was immediately hooked, the philosophy of Clean resonated within me.

It was now 2007, and David was living and working from Caitlin and Shaun Hotchkiss' home. Even though he was working closely with Shaun at this time, he was looking for someone to directly work alongside him to assist in modelling and cataloguing his latest work and developments in Emergent Knowledge.

Due to my circumstances at the time, I had the honour of Caitlin proposing this opportunity to myself, and I began working with David in the latter part of 2007. Here began a journey of discovery that would form the kernel of my development and work for the next 12 years (and, it still appears at this time, well beyond this!).

We spent some time together in Liverpool (UK) to discuss how we would be working, along with specifying the intended end goals of our working relationship.

Our first step on this adventure was to drive to France and record David's presentations and training that were lined up there at Jennifer de Gandt's beautiful home and training centre in La Bouvetière, Normandy.

David and I then spent our time in France, where, in between his training and therapy sessions, we began to codify his Emergent Knowledge patterns into a format that was to be universally transferable. My technical experience in digital networking systems aligned perfectly with the work David was presenting at the time. Thus the networking and data transfer metaphors and terminology became part of this formatting.

At the end of 2007, he left for the United States, and we remained in contact, discussing his projects and what would happen on his return. Unfortunately, in January 2008, I received a call from Steven Saunders to inform me that David had died of a heart attack. On hearing this terrible news I knew that the work we had done together up to that point could not lie dormant on my PC and in my notebooks.

On the Loss of David

During our time in France, I'd been introduced to Philip Harland where we had discussed at length his project of writing a book on David's patterning of 'Six'. On reconnecting with Philip the ideal opportunity to share our experience and knowledge opened up, together we produced the Powers of Six website http://www.powersofsix.com to share some of the fundamentals of my work with

David and his own, along with the additional intention of promoting Philip's upcoming book of the same title.

We co-wrote and published several articles together in Re-Source magazine and also co-presented a session on The Iterative Pattern of Emergence at the first Clean Conference in June 2008 - 'Roots and Fruits of Emergent Knowledge - The Joy of Six!'

At this conference I attended a short practical session on Emergence presented by Steven down in the depths of the Quaker building. This session was attended by three people, myself, Steven and another guest. I accepted the offer of having Steven run a short Emergent process on me to show the use of iteration and a Clean Space 'Turning' technique. This session brought me to a previously unknown memory (a defining moment) of being about 9 months old in a cot.

This Wounded Child recovery had a deep impact on my sense of self and it took several months for my system to settle down; however, the shift and recovery placed me in a very different and interesting space (see, Emergence a poem I wrote on the day.)

Nine months later in March 2009, I attended a Holigral retreat in Cornwall where Steven unveiled his own fully redesigned 'Whirly-Gig'. He had removed the rather dangerous operation of using three-rings down to a much safer single-ring and, through an ingenious engineering design of how all three planes of rotation work, its new design maintained all six degrees of freedom. This machine is known as 'The Ark-Angle David'.

The Ark-Angle David

My passion for sharing and evolving the knowledge I had received from David and Steven has never diminished. The Powers of Six website was further developed to include a self-processing feature called 'The Iterator', where visitors are able to explore an issue through the application of some basic and more advanced EK processes through a private online interface. This also provided me with a platform to develop and evolve my own projects and processes.

In parallel with the Powers of Six site I created the website http://www.self-alignment.com to offer a more thorough description of Grovian Emergent Knowledge as David and I had formulated it, along with an intensive 7-day personal journey process which was created out of the final material that David was presenting prior to his death.

I have ventured into several experimental projects over the years such as creating the board game 'And...', with its associated website http://www.gameofstories.com. These fun and interesting side projects pop up every now and again as connections are made.

During all of this time, I have trained and utilised the models of Emergence with students and clients.

Coming up to Present Time

In 2015 Steven decided to transition, to become Pam Saunders, integrating her full feminine self into her working, home and social life.

Sadly, in 2016 Philip Harland and I couldn't come to an agreement about how the Powers of Six website would be managed and we settled this partnership. I still own and continue to maintain and develop the Powers of Six website with new processes, articles and videos. It is my intention that this material, and that provided on Self-Alignment, will always be free to access, and may be shared and developed upon under the Open Source philosophy.

On 8th January 2018, I was gifted the opportunity to talk about my time with David at a beautiful online event *'Remembering David Grove'*, celebrating his life, 10 years after we lost him. The recording of this event is available at www.facebook.com/RememberingDavidGrove/videos

This book is my first in offering my own developments and interpretations of what I have learned from David and Pam. I am gracious of this gift. I'm fortunate to be able to share this with you.

www.ingramcontent.com/pod-product-compliance
Ingram Content Group UK Ltd.
Pitfield, Milton Keynes, MK11 3LW, UK
UKHW021052270726
13967UKWH00012B/585